IN DEFENSE OF THE ALIEN

Volume XI

*Implementing the Immigration Reform
and Control Act of 1986, Current Legislative Initiatives,
Refugees, Migration Policy: Health and Education*

IN DEFENSE OF THE ALIEN
Volume XI

*Implementing the Immigration Reform
and Control Act of 1986, Current Legislative Initiatives
Refugees, Migration Policy: Health and Education*

Proceedings of the 1988
Annual National Legal Conference
On Immigration and Refugee Policy

Edited by Lydio F. Tomasi

1989
Center for Migration Studies
New York

CMS is an education non-profit institute founded in New York in 1964 committed to encourage and facilitate the study of the sociodemographic, economic, historical, political, legislative and pastoral aspects of human migration and refugee movements. CMS organizes an annual national legal conference on immigration and refugee policy, the proceedings of which are published in a volume series entitled **IN DEFENSE OF THE ALIEN**. *This text represents the Eleventh Volume of that series.*

IN DEFENSE OF THE ALIEN
VOLUME XI
*Implementing the Immigration Reform
and Control Act of 1986, Current Legislative Initiatives,
Refugees, Migration Policy: Health and Education*

First Edition

Copyright © 1989 by

The Center for Migration Studies of New York, Inc.
209 Flagg Place
Staten Island, New York 10304-1199

ISBN 0-934733-38-4
ISSN 0275-634X

Library of Congress Catalog Number: 89-877
Printed in the United States of America

CONTENTS

Introduction

THE urgency for the kind of analytical fora provided by the Annual National Legal Conference on Immigration and Refugee Policy was underlined by the emotional reactions witnessed over the past year to immigration policy, ethnicity and what it means to be American.

"Although the [immigration reform] debate can be framed in the cool language of economics and demographics, immigration remains a highly emotional subject, with immigration policy a window into the national psyche."[1]

The emotional flows are stirred by the changing flows of immigration to this country and by the state of flux in which U.S. immigration policy resides.

"There were 1,757 legal immigrants from Ireland in 1986 ... and 5,711 from Italy, compared with 66,753 from Mexico and 61,492 from the Philippines." Asia and Latin America contribute nearly 90 percent of the more than half a million people entering the U.S. each year as legal immigrants. As of January, there were 2.2 million pending petitions from people wishing to emigrate to the U.S. - six percent more than the year before. Indochinese refugees continue to arrive at a rate of more than 50,000 a year, and the number of refugees from other areas - particularly Soviet Armenia - increases markedly.

Yet, this is the history of the making of Americans - with some differences. While in 1890 and 1910 the foreign-born population as percent of the total U.S. population reached fifteen percent, in 1980 this figure is only six percent.

Meanwhile, on the policy side of the fence, the "national origin" quotas of the 1920s was replaced by "family reunification" in the 1965 immigration law. Now, family preference is derided by some as "nepotism" and there is a push toward job skills and English-language ability (Bill S.2104). "This is bound to generate considerable debate, putting the focus on the often-overlooked social aspects of immigration."[2]

A broader debate encompasses not only a fresh look at the criteria by which the country chooses its future citizens, but also a vigorous effort (codified in the bill sponsored by Representative Barney Frank) to repeal the exclusionary provisions of the 36-year-old McCarran-Walter Act.

The ambivalence that this immigrant society has always felt toward immigration is reflected in the complexities of the current debate, which also includes refugees. Thus, for example, the Moakley-DeConcini legislation is defended as addressing an issue of justice for the refugees of El Salvador and Nicaragua and, on the other hand, it is denounced as faulty for not offering the same protection to refugees from Guatemala. Also, the refugee aid system seems in crisis. Critics are questioning whether workfare programs for refugees are better managed by private agencies or by state and local governments.

Continuing its eleven-year tradition, the CMS National Legal Conference on Immigration and Refugee Policy looked at immigration not "as a problem to be solved" but "as a phenomenon to be coped with": the historical and ever renewed challenge of the United States. Specifically, the 1988 Conference focused on the implementation of the Immigration Reform and Control Act, on current legislative initiatives, and on the impact of immigration on American society with regard to health and education.

Of the IRCA's components, the legalization program proved to be one of the most debated. The alien amnesty deadline, many contend, should have been extended both "...because of the good job the INS has done" and "...because of the poor job the INS has done".[3] Considering that about 3.5 million undocumented aliens do not qualify for the amnesty program, others say that the 1986 legislation has not resolved the crisis in undocumented aliens. Charges of civil rights abuses on the border by Customs and INS[4], and of discrimination against Hispanics have given rise to calls for clarification of internal agency policies and the limitation of agents' discretionary powers.

These and other issues related to IRCA's implementation are discussed in the first two sections of the Conference Proceedings.

The focus of Section III is on current congressional inititatives to revamp the legal immigration system. It also includes an analysis of the status of recommendations of the Select Commission on Immigration and Refugee Policy concerning legal immigration, the future of the fifth preference, and representation of aliens in administrative proceedings.

The changing situtations in today's refugee flows and the integration of refugees are some of the issues discussed in Section IV. In particular, this Section focuses on the new asylum regulations and the issues they raise about due process.

The Fifth Section examines the increasing health problems engendered by both the migrant lifestyles and IRCA regulations. It also analyzes the impact of the new immigration legislation on education.

The Conference Organizing Committee is grateful to the numerous excellent panelists as well as to all those who contributed to the success of the Conference with their suggestions and participation. The Committee is also grateful to the Center for Immigrant and Population Studies of the College of

Staten Island, CUNY, the Migrant Health Program, H.H.S., The National Italian American Foundation, the National Council of the Churches of Christ, the Protestant Episcopal Church, HIAS, and the Lutheran Council in the USA for contributing toward the expenses of the Conference.

Lydio F. Tomasi
Center for Migration Studies

FOOTNOTES

[1] Greenhouse, L., "Immigration Bill: Looking for Skills and Good English", *The New York Times*, April 10, 1988, E5.

[2] Massey, D.S., "Immigration Adjustments Ignore the Chain Effects of Family Eligibility", *The Los Angeles Times*, April 6, 1988.

[3] Meissner, D. J., Pitts III, W. and V. K. Slaughter, *The Christian Science Monitor*, April 11, 1988, Page 12.

[4] Epstein, N., "U.S. Border Agents Charged with Rights Abuse", *The Christian Science Monitor*, April 13, 1988.

PART I

IMPLEMENTING THE IMMIGRATION REFORM AND CONTROL ACT OF 1986

1

Immigration Reform:
Results and Prospects[1]

ALAN C.NELSON
Commissioner, U.S. Immigration and Naturalization Service

IT's been my pleasure to be with you at several of these conferences and, again, I extend my compliments for putting together a lot of important issues. A lot of us probably have seen or heard the Virginia Slims commercial that says, "You've Come a Long Way, Baby". I think that's a pretty good description of what has happened in Immigration in the past several years with the development of the Immigration Reform and Control Act (IRCA), and more recently with a focus on legal immigration. Immigration has always been an important issue in this country. Now it has become a front page issue and generally for the good.

"You've come a long way, baby", also applies to the Immigration and Naturalization Service. (INS). I think we can properly get a lot of credit, even from people we deal with regularly who don't always agree on issues. If you heard the debate yesterday in the House, or last week before the Senate Subcommittee, or a few weeks ago before the House Subcommittee, you know even the critics by and large have acknowledged that the INS has done a very fair, effective, efficient, and reasonable job in implementing IRCA and the general provisions of the law. I think that's proper and I accept those compliments for a job well done, not in the sense of thinking, "We've got it all covered", but quite to the contrary.

This reminds me of Winston Churchill — and there are a lot of Churchill stories, but this one will help me make the point. Churchill was well known, as you know, for smoking his big cigars and enjoying a good quantity of brandy and scotch and other liquids. He was visited at one time by a temperance group and he met them in a fairly large room. They said, "Mr. Prime Minister, we understand that you drink a lot of brandy. In fact, we believe that if all the brandy you had drunk was poured into this room it would come up to your knees." He looked at these people and he looked at the floor and he looked at the ceiling, and he said, "Oh yes, so much accomplished, but so much more to be done." I think that's very true in immigration also. We can be proud, all of us, whether we are on one side of an issue or another, of the progress we've made on these issues. They've been dramatic.

Let me turn now to the issues themselves. I'm going to hit on several themes to give you a little overview of some thoughts, ideas, challenges in some of the areas you'll be dealing with during this conference. Let's talk first about legal immigration.

We spent most of the past six or seven years dealing with illegal immigration. We passed a bill two years ago that by all objective accounts is a good bill, a balanced bill, and is working well. That doesn't mean it's perfect or that it solves all the problems. We know it won't, but we think it's the right bill. I'll come back to that a little later. But let's talk about legal immigration.

We've had a number of changes over our history, but it's been a long time since Congress or the Administration has effectively dealt with legal immigration. The Select Commission spent a lot of time on that subject seven or eight years ago. A lot of recommendations were made but they've largely been on hold for one reason or another while we've dealt with the issue of illegal immigration. Now that we've got the legislation to control illegal immigration, I think it's the perfect time to really make some dramatic strides toward reform of legal immigration.

We all are aware, of course, of the Senate action. The Kennedy-Simpson Bill passed by the slim margin of 88 to 4. I think it surprised a lot of people, either pleasantly or unpleasantly, but I think it indicates how a few powerful forces — particularly in this case Kennedy and Simpson — can effectively move something. Now there is the question, "What will the House do?" I am pleased that Congressman Rodino has indicated he will go forward and have hearings. He has instructed the staff of the Immigration Subcommittee which he chairs to get to work on options, not any particular one, but to deal with the issue appropriately.

Likewise, as many of you know, we in the Administration have a similar feeling about legal immigration reform. Now's the right time, in the last year of an Administration, to work on it. After all, we've worked a lot on the subject already, we know a lot about it. So we've come forward with our best effort, our best shot at a legal immigration reform proposal. It's working its way up to the White House for formal approval, but it's getting good marks so far, and we have shared the concept with members of the Congress in both houses, and with a number of you knowledgeable people in the private sector. As a matter of fact, some of the people I've talked to told me they were very concerned because many of our traditional adversaries like a lot of the things we're talking about in the INS proposed bill and that should scare us a little. I know even MALDEF, and a few other similar organizations who have looked at it, have had positive response to what we're talking about.

We don't claim to have the answers to everything, but I think we've got a good theme in this Administration bill. Again, it is still in the developmental process, but we're talking openly about the concepts.

One thing that we all ought to be proud of is that immigration has been, and clearly should remain, a bipartisan issue. I think we have worked very well between the Congress and the Executive Branch and the interest groups. Even though we might disagree a lot, we might fight like cats and dogs, we've made progress, we've worked together, and it's very important that we continue that way. I think Congressman Rodino sees that and we're hoping the House will move forward. If they pass a bill this year, great, that would be fine. If they don't, at least they can get a good solid foundation to move forward next year, because no matter who the President is, or who is in the next Congress, this is an issue that we need to deal with.

Let me talk a little bit about a couple of the provisions without going into detail and maybe it will come up later in discussions. We have some packets of material that are ready to go out so we'll be sharing those.

We think the overall concept of the Kennedy-Simpson Bill is pretty good. It's a good start, but we don't think it's a finished product. The idea of an independent category as a balance to the family category, we think is solid. We don't want to take away from the family, nobody does, but the balancing is a proper way to go, and we think it is a good start. One thing we do strongly believe, and I think most of you would concur in, is that the current level of 600,000 legal immigrants is a good and reasonable number. In fact, it might even be increased, particularly if we can see evidence that the illegal flow is leveling off or decreasing. So, our basic position is to keep high levels and maybe even go higher.

One reason for going higher, at least for the time being, is to deal with the backlogs of visa applicants. It's a serious problem because the backlogs themselves generate reasons for illegal immigration. Frankly, Kennedy-Simpson doesn't deal with that effectively. We think one of the provisions that needs to be added is an effective way to deal with the backlog, and to get current. We would like to see an amortization time of, say, five years to get to a current state so applicants will know whether they're going to make it or not within a year or two. I think that would be very healthy.

Another thing that hasn't really been addressed is the focus on citizenship. When you think about it, what is the purpose of immigration? To be effective, shouldn't immigrants come to this country to become assimilated in our society and to become full partners? There is no better way to do that really than to go the full route to citizenship. So, we think there ought to be more emphasis on citizenship as a criteria for immigration policy. One thing we'd do is consider reducing the time to become a citizen from five years to three years. The other is to make it more of an incentive of citizenship to be able to petition for relatives and others. So we encourage immigrants to become citizens to encourage further immigration, in addition to all the other reasons. And we think that is a solid kind of policy.

So, in brief, our proposal would keep or even raise the high immigration limits, promote citizenship, and reduce visa backlogs. As for consultation on other increases, we think the concept is good — a little bit like the refugee policy. That's where we need to look at the impact of illegal immigration. If it's dropping, maybe we can increase the number of legal arrivals. But if illegal entries stay up, we might have to keep legal numbers down.

I think that's the whole theme of our immigration law. Some people have attacked IRCA as an anti-immigration bill. It's nothing of the kind. It's a *pro*-immigration bill. By protecting the heritage of legal immigration, it means to assure that it continues. When legal immigration is undercut by illegal, as we've seen recently with almost as many people coming in illegally as legally, it tends to be seen as part of the problem. There's the danger that the American public might just say, "Enough" and want to really cut back on all immigration. We need to keep driving toward that single and generally accepted goal of controlling illegal entries to protect legal immigration.

So, I would hope all of you, no matter what your thinking is, would push forward together. Let's have hearings in the House. Let's look at different options. If we can put together a good bipartisan package, it would be an outstanding achievement for both the Reagan Administration and the Congress. If not, at least we set a foundation for the future. I urge you to spend some time and thought on it, to think hard about what you want in a legal immigration bill, and move it down the track.

Let me shift to another subject,and that's welfare reform. You might have read in the paper today that the Senate Finance Committee passed out a welfare reform bill. I consider myself a kind of expert, if there can be such a thing, on that. As some of you know, I worked for Governor Reagan in California and in 1971, I was an active player in the development, negotiation, and passage of the California Welfare Reform Plan. As I've said to many, if you had to pick one issue that propelled Ronald Reagan to the White House, it might well have been his action as Governor in getting that welfare reform plan because it raised the grants to the needy, it made the system more efficient, it got people moving toward employment or into employment, and it also had a way of checking the status to be sure that only eligible people got on the rolls. It's a good program that's worked well.

Now, some 16 or 17 years later, we are still saying "Yes, we ought to get people off welfare into jobs". But what has Congress done? Even people in the Administration? They've done a lot of tallking. Job training and education are valid, but how many people are being put into jobs? Not too many so we've still got a real problem here. It's going to get worse. One thing that irritates me the most in the debate about immigration is the argument against doing anything about illegal immigration "because no American will take those jobs". I'd say in most cases that's pure poppycock. To begin with, most employers who habitually hire illegals just want to continue their low labor costs and substandard conditions. True, there are situations where it is difficult to get domestic workers into some jobs. We have to ask why. Often it is because of our benefit structure.

Here, the nexus between immigration reform and welfare reform still has not been identified. When you look at the opportunities this country has right now, with IRCA and employer sanctions in effect, a lot of jobs that have been held by illegal aliens can be made available to the unemployed domestic workers, and a lot of these entry level jobs, certainly the kind of jobs that can be offered to the unskilled, the disadvantaged minorities, the able-bodied people on welfare, and others who need the jobs the most. Even though we have a pretty good unemployment rate, we still have a lot of unemployment, particularly among minority workers. Here is the opportunity to focus on jobs that have been held, or would have been held, by illegal aliens and to find unemployed citizens or legal aliens to fill them.

There are a couple of things we've done at INS, and I ask you as citizens to judge whether government shouldn't do more things like this. First, we develop an employer relations program. A new Assistant Commissioner was set up in our organization to work with employers, unions and labor groups, community groups and others, with this theme: Let's get legal workers into these jobs. We're not in the job placement business, but we can be a catalyst. And your organizations can do even more. A lot of you in the QDEs, in Hispanic or other interest groups, have not done enough in this area. You ought to get more involved. Here is a great opportunity for you now and in the future to join with us or work on your own to get qualified citizens and legal aliens, refugees that are here legally, into these jobs. If you do, together we can solve several problems at once. We can really make some strides toward helping the unemployed and reforming welfare. We can find out if there is any truth to "no American will take these jobs," American meaning citizen or legal alien here. To the extent that's true, it's because our welfare system has developed an unfortunate dependecy that is difficult to break, but we need to try.

I also mentioned the checking of status. You're familiar with the SAVE program. Probably a lot of you don't like the idea, but when you think of what SAVE is, again this comes right out of Ronald Reagan's 1971 Welfare Reform Program; very simple. As I say, raise grants on the one hand, then be sure that those who apply are qualified.

Just about every program, whether health, labor, education, agriculture, whatever, has a requirement in their law right now that if you're an illegal alien you don't get the benefits. But they don't check it very well, I'll tell you that. SAVE gives all the entitlement programs the ability to check alien status because INS is the only organization with aliens' records. We can check and say, "Yes, that person is here legally," or "No, that person is not." And there is a fail-safe system so nobody is cut off from their benefits unfairly. It's a solid program. We now have 22 states signed up, voluntarily, on this program. We'll probably have another eight or 10 within the next few months. It's working. By October, it will be generally implemented. We now have a verification system that's working well.

This isn't a philosophical issue, it's a good government issue, and there is no reason why illegal aliens who are not qualified for these programs ought to get the benefits. If they're qualified, they can get them; if they're illegal, they cannot. Again, this is part of welfare reform. I think all of you at this Conference, as you proceed with your continuing efforts in immigration reform, should keep this idea of welfare reform in mind. Both reforms go together for the benefit of those here legally and the benefit of our legal immigration system.

Let me talk a little bit about refugees. I'll just touch on a couple of issues here that I'd like you to think about.

One is the welfare dependency problem. It really is a shame when a person comes in as a refugee with the tremendous desire to be in this free country and then ends up on welfare — sometimes because our system encourages it. We have to work together — the interest groups, the churches, the QDEs and voluntary agencies, and the government — to break this welfare dependency cycle. I remember four years ago, I was in Thailand. I went to one of the refugee processing centers and I was quite surprised and frankly shocked when I heard the State Department representative, who was instructing the people who were going to come to the States say something like, "Well, you have two options. One is you go to work and the other is you can go on welfare." That was about what they were saying. Surely there is a lot more all of us can say and do, if we're truly interested in people and in human advancement. Welfare isn't the way to go for these refugees who have a lot of talent and desire to contribute. We need to do something more than is being done.

Another factor in the refugee issue, though you may not agree, is that there are a lot of people coming in as refugees who are really immigrants. We're now twelve years from the Vietnam War, but I think there is still a lot of pressure to bring in everyone from Southeast Asia as refugees. I understand the reason for it. We are still very generous in that area. The important thing is to be objective and to be able to make a distinction. And if there is a special reason to bring people in as refugees— for example, currently the Armenians in Russia — most people would acknowledge it. By and large, the Armenians are not typical political refugees, but we're going to bring a lot of them in and properly so. I'm throwing this out as an issue again for you to discuss. Maybe, either under the Refugee Act or the new immigration bill, we can have a special category for x number of refugees to be used by the government for special needs to bring in a group of Armenians, or a group of Vietnamese, or whomever else, without distorting the refugee definition.

We have to be careful because it's easy to play around with it a little bit. Like the problem of illegal versus legal immigration, if we start undercutting the basic premise of "fear of persecution" by bootlegging a lot of immigrants into the refugee program, we hurt both the refugee program and the immigrant program. Everyone involved in this as an expert needs to think hard about finding some human solutions without distorting the legal processes.

We also have to watch numbers games in that area, too. We've had some discussions, but we need to focus more on the issue of reviewing refugee denials. A lot of political power comes to play with too much review and re-review. After two or three reviews, 90 percent are accepted up front, right off the bat, another couple percent are picked up on subsequent more thorough reviews, with all the agencies participating. And there is still some pressure to take more just to meet the numbers. It's usually covered with the argument that we haven't been fair. I think that's ridiculous. We've got to look at the big picture when we're taking 90 percent of a group. We've got to have a selection criteria and an honest application of the standards.

I know many of you support the Moakley-DeConcini bill to grant extended voluntary departure (EVD) to certain aliens denied refugee status. The bill probably will be coming up in the Senate again. All I can say is, "Think hard. What are you accomplishing with EVD?" It sounds good and would let a lot of people stay.

As I've said on other occasions, I was at the University of California in the 50s and more than ten years after World War II there were still a lot of temporary buildings left over from the war, still in use. And the president of the university was sometimes asked by visitors, "Why do you still have all these temporary buildings around?" His reply was, "There is nothing so permanent as a temporary building". I'd say the same thing about refugees or immigrants — nothing is so permanent as a temporary status. Once they're here, they're going to stay. That is a practical fact of life. So, if we're talking about EVD, we'd better be prepared that people are going to come, they're going to stay, and they're not going to return. Maybe that's all right, but you can't say, "Well, they'll just be here for a while, for safe haven. and then go back."

Remember also the foreign policy aspects of EVD. Clearly it's a foreign policy issue. Under objective analysis, EVD clearly undercuts our immigration policy and our refugee policy. It's really a foreign policy in wolf and sheep's clothing. Even though you might like and support Moakley-DeConcini, you would have to acknowledge that fact. And objectivity is important for the long term because immigration is an issue we all want to deal with as a long term issue.

I thought it was very interesting to have seen the report on television (in April) about President Reagan and former presidents Ford and Carter talking to groups of school children. At the end of the program President Reagan said to the kids, "You know, one thing about Americans. We're unique. You might move to Germany and live there permanently, but you're never going to be German. The same is true if you move to Japan, you might be allowed to live there, but you'll never be Japanese. But when you come here to America and live here, you can become an American." I agree that's unique with us and that's another reason why we ought to do more with our whole citizenship as part of our immigration policy.

Let me get back to IRCA and the impact that it has made. We've all heard a lot of discussion about it, a lot of testimony, but thinking objectively even a few of our critics have to admit it has been a success. Remember that IRCA was primarily an enforcement bill. It had a balance with legalization and special agricultural provisions, but it was intended to deal with the serious problem of controlling illegal immigration. We shouldn't lose sight of that.

The enforcement provisions of IRCA can be reduced to four basic elements: border enforcement, employer sanctions, entitlements, and criminal aliens. First, the border is being strengthened largely through the budget with more manpower. Second, job market enforcement ends with employer sanctions but begins with voluntary compliance and hiring legal workers. The purpose of IRCA is not to penalize employers but to prevent job opportunities for illegal aliens. Third point, in the entitlements market, SAVE keeps illegal aliens from getting benefits to which they're not entitled. And fourth, interior enforcement is targeted against aliens who commit serious crimes, such as aggravated felonies, to identify them, aprehend them, and make sure they are properly deported. Those four elements are working. It's only a beginning, of course, but we're pleased with the results so far.

In border enforcement, we're moving up the numbers of agents. We're also extremely involved in the drug war and very proud of our accomplishments. INS has seized over half of all the drugs seized on the southern border. That's fascinating when you consider we get no money outside of the immigration bill and that it's just tied into our regular function. But contraband and illegal aliens have often gone together. And interdiction of both has been working well. We have had roughly a 30 percent drop in apprehensions. We think that's a good sign. It crept up a little bit in January, February and March 1988 but is still 20 percent below the 1986 figures. We think that's a positive sign, although no one wants to get trapped in a numbers game. They are one indicator that border enforcement is beginning to work.

For employer sanctions, I think properly we have to get very high marks. We went through a very open process of regulation and development of forms and procedures. We hear very little complaint about the handbooks or the forms. They're working. We've spent a tremendous amount of time on education and voluntary compliance on our own initiative. Congress didn't tell us to do this. We did it. We're going to have made over a million visits of employers; one on one, to tell them what the law's about and hearq about their concerns and problems.

Of course we also have issued many citations and even several fines for obvious violations. The early fines largely have been paid or settled, which I think is a sign we've done it pretty well. We think the process will continue to work well. We remain open to your suggestions or comments. As of June 1, 1988, warning citations are no longer required. We're exploring now what we should do with respect to employer visits, citations and so forth, and we're looking at the different options. Clearly we're going to continue to promote a high level of voluntary compliance but we'll impose sanctions when necessary.

The SAVE system, I've mentioned, is beginning to work well. We've already kept off about 50,000 ineligible aliens and saved millions of dollars. There is a lot more to come. It's good immigration and welfare reform.

The criminal alien issue doesn't get as much attention, but should. Why should any country allow people who came in illegally, committed violent crimes, and served time in prison, to get back out in the street and commit more crimes before we're able to track them down and deport them. Other countries deport Americans who commit crimes, and properly so. It ought to be a two-way street. That's the whole theme. I don't think anybody favors keeping people here who clearly are deportable for their criminal activities. So that's beginning to work well.

As for legalization and Special Agricultural Workers (SAW), I think we all know the numbers. We've done well and we'll continue to do well. We're in a surge mode right now, up through May 4. The SAW program is at about 400,000 as of mid-April and will continue through November. Regular legalization has brought roughly 1.2 million so far but we expect another 100,000 to come in before the deadline. So we'll be at 1.7 million or so, maybe better than that, when you look at al the programs together. We play these number games, but remember, the real purpose is taking people from illegal status and giving them the opportunity to be here legally and move down the track to permanent residency and citizenship. So with legalization, SAW, Cuban-Haitian adjustment, the registry program, and although not part of IRCA, the Mikulski EVD program, we will have reduced our illegal alien population by over two million. And then if we add the derivative relatives that flow in after that over the years, we'll be adding another million or more. So we're going to be talking about three million or more people that will have been converted from an illegal to a legal status. As we all know, the totals of the other countries of the world that have had these programs amounts to about 450,000. so we're already four times that. When we add it all together, we'll be five, six, seven times that total. So I don't think anybody can argue with the success of the program.

Now, if we talk about extension of this program, I will only make it clear our position has been very explicit. We think this program has worked well, but extension is bad. The fact that it passed the House (in April) is one strike out of three before the matter is resolved. We do not expect an extension to take place. The one message that all of us should carry to any qualified aliens who haven't yet come forward is "Apply now!" Don't depend on any chance to file after May 4 for the regular legalization program. It would be a disservice not to pass that message on to any people out there who might be sitting back thinking an extension is going to happen. So no matter how strongly you support an extension don't waste your efforts lobbying for it at the expense of getting the word out to those people who might be eligible. We're thinking this program is working well. We're pleased with the cooperative efforts of all the groups involved. We all ought to be pleased. But let's be sure that we push it vigorously here to the end so we get everybody who's eligible to come forward in time.

Let me tell one last Churchill story, which is allegedly a true story. Churchill and George Bernard Shaw were quite adversarial in their relationship. Both were pretty strong-willed. So at one point Shaw sent Churchill two tickets to an opening of a new play that he had written, and the letter transmitting the tickets read as follows, "Dear Mr. Churchill: Enclosed are two tickets for the opening of my new play for you and a friend, if you have one." Sometimes it seems INS is in that category. But Churchill, not to be outdone, wrote back and said, "Dear Mr. Shaw, I really appreciate the courtesy of your sending me these tickets to your play. Unfortunately, my calendar won't permit me to attend the opening performance. However, I would very much like to attend the second performance, if there is one." Thank you.

FOOTNOTES

[1]   This article is the edited transcript of a speech delivered by Commissioner Nelson on April 21, 1988, at the CMS Eleventh National Legal Conference on Immigration and Refugee Policy in Washington, D.C.

2

Immigration Reform and Agricultural Labor

WILLIAM SLATTERY
INS Assistant Commissioner for Legalization

THE Immigration Reform Act is working. The best evidence is the sharp decline in the number of people attempting illegal entry across our Southern border. INS Border Patrol apprehensions at the border are down nearly 40 percent since the bill became law in November 1986.

Recently there have been concerns in the Western United States that there have been and may be a shortage of agricultural workers in the harvest months ahead. We all recognize and appreciate the vital role agriculture plays in our nation's economy. No one wants crop losses due to worker shortages. The evidence is mixed on the extent of the actual or potential labor shortage, but U.S. Government representatives have met with growers, Congressional representatives and others to explore ways to assure an adequate agricultural workforce.

Contained in the new Immigration Reform and Control Act are special provisions for agricultural workers, which the nation's growers worked very hard to achieve. By effectively using these provisions, the labor needs of agriculture can be met without undercutting the new immigration law.

Following are approaches the Federal Government is taking and further actions that will be initiated to ensure an adequate supply of agricultural labor. These have been discussed in detail with a group of Senators and Congressmen in several recent meetings on Capitol Hill.

EXISTING PROCEDURES IN PLACE

Processing in United States

Currently there are 107 legalization offices which accept Special Agricultural Worker (SAW) applicants. These offices were staffed and opened on June 1, 1987, to accept up to 16,650 applications per day. INS has designated 157 agriculturally oriented Qualified Designated Entities (QDEs) to assist SAW applicants in applying for legalization status. Qualified applicants can receive temporary work authorization on the day they file their applications. Through June 24, 1987, 10,300 SAW applications have been filed in the United States.

H-2A Processing

The Immigration Reform and Control Act of 1986 (IRCA) established a new streamlined temporary agricultural program - H-2A. This program is available to growers. To date no H-2A applications have been filed in the Western states.

Emergency H-2A Processing

In areas which may suffer emergency agricultural labor shortages during periods of peak labor demand, the Department of Labor and INS are prepared to process employer applications for temporary agricultural labor certification and petitions for H-2A classification on an expedited basis, provided that such employers can meet all labor standards and protections required under the H-2A program, such as wages and housing. In such instances the entire stateside H-2A process can be completed in one week.

INS Emergency Utilization of H-2A

Where the Department of labor may deny a Section 216(e)(2) redetermination application, based on its finding that American labor is available, an employer can file an appeal along with its H-2A petition to INS. The petition can be approved if the employer establishes to INS' satisfaction that domestic labor is not available.

Processing in Mexico

Currently, SAW applicants who are in Mexico must apply at the Overseas Processing Post established at the U.S. Embassy in Mexico City. The applicants are notified of their interview appointment, and if found eligible, they proceed to the United States and are given the six-month work authorization card. The procedure then follows the normal processing used for applicants in the USA. As of June 24, 4,000 SAW applications have been distributed buy the Embassy in Mexico City.

NEW PROCEDURES TO BE IMPLEMENTED BY THE GOVERNMENT

The Administration, in cooperation with key members of Congress and agricultural organizations, will pursue the following additional steps to avoid any potential crop losses in the 1987 growing season:

SAW Processing in United States

Legalization Offices

To maximize SAW applications, legalization offices are prepared to open evenings and weekends to accommodate the scheduling of agricultural workers.

Rural Processing

To assist SAW applicants in remote areas, processing will be conducted by utilizing 40 INS mobile vans. This is in addition to the 107 Legalization Offices noted above.

Public Information

INS is expanding its existing public information campaign in agricultural areas, informing potential SAW applicants about the legalization program. INS will spend nearly $1 million on advertising and publicity to increase awareness of the SAW and H-2A programs in both the United States and Mexico. The INS advertising agency is currently buying radio time in both the U.S. and Mexico to publicize the program. In addition, written flyers will be distributed to encourage SAW participation among eligible workers and to encourage grower associations and others to pursue actively their responsibilities to identify, locate and assist eligible workers to apply.

Qualified Designated Entities

INS will work with agricultural QDEs to expedite their review process so that SAW applications may be filed in a timely manner.
Such QDEs must significantly increase their efforts with growers and workers to file applications.

Grower Associations

INS will work with grower associations to help them assist workers to document their eligibility and complete applications. Grower associations and labor organizations must significantly increase their efforts with growers and workers to file applications.

Interagency Clearing House

USDA, DOL, and INS will coordinate efforts to assist growers facing labor shortages. Grower associations and others will be assisted in carrying out their responsibilities in identifying eligible workers, preparing SAW applications for former workers, contacting former workers abroad through grower associations operating overseas and expediting the processing of H-2A applications. USDA Agricultural Extension Agents will head interagency teams in various rural areas starting in June 1987.

May 1, Cutoff Date

The date before which a SAW must have entered the United States to be eligible to file an application in the United States will be moved from May 1, 1987 to the date on which border processing at Calexico was initiated (June 26, 1987). This will permit SAW eligibles in the United States to remain here to file applications while those outside the United States will be able to avail themselves of expedited processing at overseas processing posts and the Calexico border port. By retaining a cutoff date there will be no inducement to prospective overseas applicants to enter the United States illegally.

Border Processing

A SAW border processing center opened on June 26, 1987, at Calexico, California, as described below.

PROCESSING OF SAW APPLICANTS FROM MEXICO

Processing in the Interior of Mexico

Application forms and accompanying instructions will be available at all consulates and at the nine consular agencies in Mexico by July 1. SAW processing under the temporary emergency procedures will be expanded in the interior of Mexico to include the acceptance and processing of applications at the consulates in Monterrey and Hermosillo in addition to the consular section at the Embassy in Mexico City. Possible expansion to the remaining non-border consulates, i.e., Guadalajara, Mazatlan, and Merida will be considered depending on the volume of applicants in the interior.

Any staffing difficulties encountered by the Department of State will be communicated to the INS, which will make available Spanish speaking staff. Such officers will be available within 10 days of notification.

Physicals

During this period of expedited processing, SAW applicants will be accepted without required physicals. The physical exam will be deferred, not waived. Work authorizations will be granted and the application will be placed in normal processing as the record of medical examination is received.

Border Processing

SAW eligibles residing in Mexican border states only will temporarily be permitted to present applications for SAW status at a border port of entry. INS legalization staff will be detailed to Calexico, California, to initiate border processing which started June 26, 1987. Other ports may be designated to conduct border processing depending on grower/applicant response. During the first 30 days, the success of this program will be monitored and expansion or termination will be considered. Such additional locations, if any, will be opened within ten days of decision.

Admission Standards

For the 1987 growing season, to assure an adequate agricultural workforce, Special Agricultural Worker (SAW) applicants will be able to gain admission to the United States immediately by filing an application and fee at an American Consulate or INS border processing site. As long as the application clearly indicates the details of their qualifying employment, the workers will be given 90 days to collect supporting documentation in the United States. These procedures will be effective July 1, 1987.

These applicants will be given permission to work during this interim period while they are assembling this additional evidence of eligibility. By the end of this period the applicant will be required to be interviewed and otherwise comply with the requirements of this program such as provision of full supportive documentation and the medical examination to receive SAW status under the law. The cooperation of growers' associations and others is required and expected in providing workers with the necessary documentation to complete the application. The Federal Government is taking this significant step as a practical and flexible solution to allow persons who are apparently qualified for SAW status to be admitted on a temporary basis for this growing season only. This action should not be perceived as a change in our legal analysis of the SAW worker program which was developed over the extensive and open regulatory process culminating in final regulations published on May 1, 1987.

Rather, this is a practical solution made in conjunction with Members of Congress to facilitate a smoother transition from widespread use of illegal workers in Western Agriculture to legal employment practices as provided in the Immigration Reform and Control Act of 1986.

Processing of H-2A Applications

Dissemination of Information of Successful H-2A Programs

INS Northern Regional commissioner James Buck is assisting Northwest Growers Association representatives obtain information on successful Idaho and Florida H-2A programs. Such information will be available to all growers nationwide. Similar efforts will be pursued in California and other areas.

ACTIONS FOR GROWERS TO PURSUE

Assistance in Mexico from Growers' Representatives

It is desirable that a limited number of representatives from U.S. growers travel to Mexico to assist in the application process for those agricultural laborers who have worked for growers in the twelve-month period ending May 1, 1986. The purpose of their presence will be to provide documentation concerning the applicant's employment and to assist in the preparation of the application at the port of entry processing facility as well as at interior consulates.

The presence of such grower's representatives in Mexico and any limitations on the types of activities they may pursue is to be discussed by the State Department with the Government of Mexico. Additionally, such representatives, prior to traveling to Mexico, should coordinate with consular officials at the U.S. Consulate in Mexico to which they are destined. Such coordination should ensure maximum orderliness in the processing procedures for targeted workers.

Efforts to Identify Eligible Workers

Extensive additional efforts by grower associations are necessary to locate eligible workers in the U.S. and overseas and assist with completing and filing applications. Only the growers and workers have the required documentation.

OTHER AVAILABLE SOURCES OF AGRICULTURAL LABOR

In addition to the special treatment Congress afforded agriculture in the Immigration Reform Act, other untapped labor sources have been successful in past situations and should be fully explored by growers and government officials. These include persons currently unemployed and/or on welfare, college and high school students on summer break, referrals from community groups and day workers who often gather at designated locations awaiting job offers.

The strong public and bi-partisan support for welfare reform, together with the need for additional workers in agriculture, provides a unique opportunity to develop both long-term and short-term programs utilizing persons currently on welfare or other benefit programs. Among the approaches that could be considered would be the development of child care centers to give welfare recipients and others the opportunity for productive employment in agriculture.

CONCLUSION

The Government has taken a number of special steps to ensure an orderly transition to the new Immigration Reform and Control Act and to avoid the prospect of crop losses due to labor shortages. The workers who qualify and the growers who alone can provide the necessary information to the workers must energetically act now.

The new immigration law is working, as is being currently demonstrated. We urge growers and others to support America by utilizing the legal labor sources provided under the new immigration law and by making a transition from previous practices of employing illegal labor.

3

Amnesty: Can We Learn a Simpler and More Generous Approach?

IRA J. KURZBAN
Kurzban, Kurzban and Weinger, P.A., Miami, Florida

THE Immigration Reform and Control Act of 1986 ("IRCA"), Pub. L. 99-603, 100 Stat. 3359 (November 6, 1986) contains three major amnesty programs — legalization under §201, Cuban-Haitian Adjustment under §202, and Special Agricultural Worker (SAW) status under §210.[1] In combination, these three programs represent the largest amnesty program ever granted in any industrialized nation in the world. By the time the last initial filing period for the last program is over on November 30, 1988, perhaps more than two and one-half million (2,500,000) people will benefit.

The size and nature of these programs alone have posed challenges to the resources, manpower, and creativity even of an organization as large and diversified as the Immigration and Naturalization Service. The three programs, because they differ in statutory and regulatory requirements, in application dates, and in the application of the standard and nature of proof to establish a claim placed extraordinary burdens on the INS to train its officers and to communicate often subtle changes in policy and practice. For these reasons, the analysis of the three programs, their administrative execution, the results and the public's reaction will be a source of inquiry for years to come not only for legal scholars but for scholars in public administration, political science, organization theory and public policy. Without the benefit of the appropriate sophisticated set of case studies on these programs, I should nevertheless like to offer some general observations as one who has participated in various stages of these programs as a commentator on the regulations, as president of the American Immigration Lawyers Association and as an attorney representing disenfranchised applicants under the regulations.

LEGALIZATION

In addressing the success of the legalization program and its implementation by INS, one must first scrutinize the underlying statute that Congress provided the agency. The statutory scheme undoubtedly contributed to INS' subsequent difficulties in the administration and implementation of the program.

At its simplest and most elegant form, legalization could have been an extended registry program that moved the date for registry to November 6, 1986 instead of January 1, 1972 (the date selected by Congress) or even January 1, 1982 (the date selected for legalization). A registry date complimentary with the employer sanctions provisions of IRCA and the passage date of the Act would have eliminated a substantial part of the problems which preceded and followed the legalization program. Registry would not have required the comparable expenditure in time, money or bureaucratic changes that accompanied legalization. Registry would not have required, for the most part, the establishment of additional offices or additional personnel. It also would have eliminated the need for a separate SAW program. Moreover, as registry does not have a cut-off date for filing, applicants would not have been forced to submit their applications by a certain date. Applicants would, therefore, have been able to file, and INS could have received, the applications in a more orderly, less frantic, pace than existed under legalization.

The congressional choice to utilize a January 1, 1982 cut-off date instead of a "date-of-the-act-" provision also had a deleterious effect on the program. By utilizing a date earlier than enactment and earlier than employer sanctions, legalization has created a new class of persons who are afraid to come out of the shadows for fear of detection. Persons who entered the United States between January 1, 1982 and November 6, 1986 are likely to live and work illegally in the United States because their employers are not subject to sanctions under the "grandfather" provision of employer sanctions. Similarly, persons who entered the United States before January 1, 1982 but did not become illegal until after that date also fall within this category. The result has been the creation of a new class of persons who will remain in an "underground" illegal status - the condition the legislation was designed to avoid. Moreover, the INS program of "family fairness" unfortunately did little to assuage these concerns. [2]

Other requirements expressed in the legalization statute also created barriers to applicants seeking temporary residency. Congress established rules of exclusion concerning three misdemeanors and one felony, public charge, continuous residency and continuous physical presence or whether or not your presence was "known to the government". Congress also established special waivers for ineligible applicants.

These problems were magnified by the interpretations which INS gave to these concepts. First, the INS defined congressional terms in ways which were contrary to long standing practice, see Gutierrez v. Ilchert, 682 F.Supp. 467, 473-75 (N.D. Cal. 1988) (striking down INS interpretation under IRCA regulations of brief, casual and innocent trips as inconsistent with INS' long standing interpretation); *Catholic Social Services, Inc. v. Meese,* 685 F.Supp. 1149 (C.D. Cal. 1988) (same). Second, INS defined terms in a manner which was plainly inconsistent with congressional intent, *see Ayuda, Inc. v. Meese,* 687 F.Supp. 650 (D.D.C. 1988) (known to the government did not mean known to INS). INS' unnecessarily narrow or plainly incorrect reading of congressional intent on these issues caused substantial confusion in the potential applicant population.

Similarly, INS' frequent changes in position on a number of critical issues discouraged and confused potential applicants. For example, INS did not provide any clear definition on how expunged convictions would be treated and whether they could bar the use of convictions which would render the applicant for amnesty ineligible. The INS' initial position was that expunged convictions could not erase an applicant's conviction thereby barring him from legalization. The last position of INS, established less than two weeks before the completion of the program accepted the opposite position. (Int. Rel. Vol. 65 No. 16, April 25, 1988 at pp. 437-38.)

In addition, the regulations, at times, reflected overly technical distinctions that made it difficult for immigration lawyers and examiners to follow and impossible for the general public to comprehend. The formal, legalistic approach was most evident in the treatment of questions concerning public charge where, ironically, the applicants were more likely to have little knowledge about the program and less access to legal assistance. One example of this approach was the definition of public cash assistance in relation to educational assistance programs for purposes of determining the applicability of the public charge bar to legalization. The Associate Commissioner's memorandum on this issue states:

> Education assistance programs are not to be considered public cash assistance as long as the funds provided are designated specifically to meet educational needs such as tuition and books; however, if the education program also provides for subsistence needs it should then be considered as public cash assistance.

While the agency may view such hairsplitting as necessary to clarify unresolved legal issues, such distinctions leave the applicant speechless if not breathless, and undoubtedly confused. A program that attempts to reach a socially and economically underground population that has marginal educational and English language skills and no legal training, is hampered by a legalistic approach. A simpler and more generous approach would be more consistent with the program's goals.

One way to overcome many of these difficulties would have been to establish a significant public campaign which focused less on legal details and, instead, urged people to come forward. A swift approval of a substantial number of applications would have sent a clear signal to applicants that the INS was concerned and ready to grant amnesty to eligible applicants. Unfortunately, the program took so long to begin sending approval notices that the positive effects that could have been derived from early approvals was lost. Similarly, INS lost an early opportunity to reach the applicant population through a public service media campaign. The media program unfortunately was too little, too late.

The INS, however, scored a major victory in the legalization program in its establishment of satellite legalizaton offices. By establishing small offices in immigrant communities, INS made the program and the agency more accessible to the public. Applicants were less intimidated by the agency when they went to a small neighborhood office instead of the centralized, "downtown" location with long lines. INS officers responded in kind and were more relaxed, professional and courteous. This positive approach should be considered on a permanent, even if limited, basis.

CUBAN-HAITIAN ADJUSTMENT ACT

The Cuban-Haitian Adjustment Act represented a triumph for Haitians who had been in the United States without status for many years. Haitian boat people began arriving in South Florida in December, 1972. Many of them remained without status in the United States until the passage of this Act. Although the Act also covers Cuban applicants, most Cuban entrants, including those from Mariel, had applied or could apply under the Cuban Refugee Adjustment Act of 1966. The success of the program therefore should be properly measured by the numbers of Haitians who were able to apply for residency under the program.

In District VI of INS, which covers the State of Florida, INS made an outstanding and successful effort to grant status to Haitian applicants as quickly as possible. Under the leadership of the District Director Perry Rivkind, the agency established a special program to address the approximately 30,000 to 40,000 applicants who sought status as Haitian entrants. To the agency's credit, it addressed these applications in an expedited program lasting only several months that caused little disruption to the rest of the district office's work. The program was conducted in a courteous, professional environment that emphasized the generous nature of the program consistent with congressional intent. As a result of these efforts well over twenty thousand Haitians have become residents and are now able to apply for citizenship and become full members of our political and economic community.

In sharp contrast to these efforts, the INS district office in New York City took a far more negative view of the process. Although there were substantial numbers of Haitian applicants in New York City, the District Director refused to establish even a limited special program to process these applicants. Indeed, many of the applicants were deprived of their right to apply for legalization because the district office did not adjudicate Haitian Adjustment applications until after the May 5, 1988 deadline for amnesty had passed. The district office also refused to deem such applications as timely filed for amnesty purposes, thereby depriving applicants of the ability to seek residency under the legalizaton program after they were denied under the Haitian Adjustment Act. The district director, in conjunction with the INS central office, also deemed legalization waivers to be unavailable to Haitian adjustment applicants despite the clear language of §202(f) of IRCA which provided that the Attorney General's authority would not be restricted by virtue of the passage of Haitian Adjustment. The result of this position is that applicants who are excludable under §212(a)(19) of the Immigraton and Nationality Act and who do not have close relatives in the United States are barred from obtaining residency under the program. These harsh and unnecessary consequences are particularly questionable here where the exclusion of Haitians on this ground is the result of changes in §212(a)(19) which occurred after the passage of IRCA, where the underlying act may have occurred many years in the past, and where the applicants are eligible for waivers under the legalization program that should be applied to this program.

The climate of harassment, intimidation and hostility faced by Haitians in New York who were seeking permanent residency under this special act was also in sharp contrast to the courteous and professional treatment they received in Florida and other places in the United States. As a result of the overtly hostile treatment Haitians received in New York City, litigation has been initiated against the district director and his staff.

The programs in New York, Florida and other districts have also posed problems for Haitians who are not registered in INS computers or for whom files do not exist. Under the Act a Haitian who "was documented" by INS is entitled to receive the benefit of adjustment to permanent residency. The legislative history of the Act was replete with references to the need that the statutory language be broadly construed in light of the Act's ameliorative purposes (see, Cuban/Haitian Adjustment, Hearing on H.R. 4853, before the Subcommittee on Immigration, Refugees and International Law of the House Committees on the Judiciary, 99th Cong. 2d Sess.) Unfortunately, there are numerous instances where no file exists, where the Haitian's alien registration number was mistakenly given to another person, or where the Haitian is not listed on INS' computer.

The legislative history of the Act recognized the problem of lost files and the lack of current documentary evidence because many files had been lost during the course of the Jean v. Nelson, 472 U.S. 846 (1985) litigation or simply as a result of the passage of time back to 1972. The agency's position on this issue has been to refuse to grant status even where the applicant presents secondary proof in the form of affidavits and live testimony. The

INS will only grant status to such persons if INS records reflect that the files had been lost or destroyed. The rejection of such applicants has caused significant hardship and deprived such persons of their rights under the Act. The Haitian Refugee Center, Inc. and other organizations have begun litigation on this issue to correct the agency's erroneous position.

SPECIAL AGRICULTURAL WORKERS PROGRAM

The Special Agricultural Workers (SAW) program is the amnesty program for persons who have engaged in agricultural labor in the United States. Similar to legalization, this program provides first for a temporary resident status and after a waiting period for permanent residency.

Under the SAW program, the Attorney General must grant temporary lawful resident status to any alien who applies for such status within the statutorily set time period (June 1, 1987 to November 30, 1988), is admissible to the United States as an immigrant, and can establish that s/he resided in the United States and performed at least 90 man-days of seasonal agricultural service in the United States during the 12-month period ending on May 1, 1986. 8 U.S.C. §1160(a)(1).

The SAW applicant has the initial burden of proving by a preponderance of the evidence that s/he has worked the 90 man-days of farm labor. 8 U.S.C. §1160(b)(3)(B)(i). A SAW applicant "can meet such burden of proof...by providing sufficient evidence of that employment as a matter of just and reasonable inference. In such a case, the burden then shifts to the Attorney General to disprove the alien's evidence with a showing which negates the reasonableness of the inference to be drawn from the evidence". 8 U.S.C. §1160(b)(3)(B)(iii). No specific kind of proof is required of SAW applicants. Congress, recognizing that standard employment records often do not exist or would be extremely difficult for many farmworkers to obtain, made the Fair Labor Standards Act ("FLSA") caselaw, applicable to SAW cases. This caselaw provides an exceptionally lenient standard of proof that allows even uncorroborated testimony alone to create a just and reasonable inference that shifts the burden of disproving that inference to the other party. (See, H.R. Conf. Rep. No. 1000, 99th Cong. 2d Sess. 97, reprinted in 1986 U.S. Code Cong. & Admin. News 5840, 5853.) INS regulations similarly provide that proof other than standard employer records, including affidavits from crewleaders and co-workers may be submitted. 8 C.F.R. §210.3(c)(3).

Despite the liberal standards envisioned by Congress, INS has applied the standard of proof in the SAW program in a way that undermines congressional intent. Because the INS has been concerned about fraud in the SAW program, it has established requirements concerning the production of documents including payroll and other employment records that farmworkers never had and could not possibly produce. By ignoring the "just and reasonable inference" to be drawn from contractor affidavits, the INS has denied

SAW applications where other employment records could not be produced. The result has been an exceptionally high denial rate in the program. As of August 4, 1988 almost 15 percent of SAW applications nationwide were denied in comparison to 1.69 percent of general legalization cases. In the Southern Region the denial rate for SAW applicants has been much higher around the 35 percent to 40 percent range. The effect of INS' practice has been to disenfranchise a significant number of persons who Congress intended to cover under the legislation.

The practice by INS of altering the standard of proof necessary to establish farmworker status inevitably led to litigation on this and other issues relating to SAW applicatons. In *Haitian Refugee Center, Inc., et al. v. Nelson, et al.,* Case No. 88-1066-Civ-Atkins (S.D. Fla. August 22, 1988) the district court entered a sweeping injunction requiring INS to readjudicate all applications where improper procedures were utilized. The court's order resulted in the review of approximately 21,000 SAW applications. A similar lawsuit has been filed in the Western District of Texas. *Arturo Ramirez-Fernandez, et al. v. Giugni, et al.,* Case No. EP-88-CA-389 (W.D. Tex. September 13, 1988).

The INS' conduct in these cases was reminiscent of its treatment of asylum claims in Haitian cases[3] and voluntary departure decisions in Salvadoran cases.[4] In its legitimate concern to ferret out fraud in the SAW program, the Service unfortunately ignored the safeguards that Congress had established to insure the impartial adjudication of farmworker claims. As it had in the Haitian and Salvadoran cases, the Service ignored the right of each applicant to an individualized determination of his or her claim. It is fortunate that the courts have remained open to correct such administrative errors.

CONCLUSION

The INS deserves great credit for its efforts to cope similtaneously with three distinct amnesty programs that involved vast numbers of people in a relatively short time period. In most instances, it carried out its task under difficult conditions set by Congress and it did so in a professional manner that accorded dignity to applicants.

We can learn a great deal from these amnesty programs for any future program of adjudications that involve a population as large as amnesty applicants. In the future, Congress should establish a simpler more generous program, if its purpose is to encourage applicants to come forward. Similarly, INS should be concerned less with hairsplitting legal distinctions than the effect that complex regulations will have on a program designed to encourage persons to come forward. Finally, the lesson to be learned from the SAW program is that each applicant must be accorded individual consideration and that the Service must be resistant to internal or external pressures that would deprive an applicant of that treatment. In an amnesty program the impulse toward generosity not the preoccupation with fraud or expeditious treatment should be the overriding concern.

FOOTNOTES

[1]   The requirements generally for each program are as follows:
1. Legalization - an applicant must have been in the United States illegally before January 1, 1982. S/he must have resided continuously in the U.S. after that date and must not otherwise be ineligible under §212(a) of the Immigration and Nationality Act ("INA") or because the person was convicted of the commission of one felony or three misdemeanors. If the applicant is successful s/he receives temporary resident status. After eighteen (18) months the applicant may apply for permanent residency.
2: Cuban Haitian Adjustment - any Cuban or Haitian who had been designated as an Entrant by the INS or who was documented by INS before January 1, 1982 is eligible for permanent residency. If the applicant entered the U.S. before January 1, 1982 on a tourist visa and was not designated a Cuban-Haitian Entrant at that time, s/he had to apply for asylum in the United States before January 1, 1982 to be eligible for this program. Certain grounds of exclusion, such as crimes of moral turpitude under §212(a)(19), would bar residency while other grounds, such as a previous order of exclusion or deportation under §212(a)(17), would not. Proposed technical amendments to this Act would eliminate the §212(a)(19) bar as well. The Cuban-Haitian Adjustment applicant, if successful, becomes a resident with a roll back date to January 1, 1982 and therefore becomes eligible for citizenship as soon as s/he obtains residency. Unlike the legalization or SAW program, Cuban-Haitian Entrants become residents without going through a temporary residency period.
3. Special Agricultural Workers - provides temporary residency to applicants who can show that they worked in agricultural labor as defined by the Secretaary of Agriculture for at least 90 man days between May 1, 1985 to May 1, 1986. Agriculture includes fruit and vegetables and perishable commodities. This program also leads to permanent residency, but the waiting time for permanent residency will depend upon the number of years that a person worked in agricultural employment before applying under the SAW program.

[2]   The family fairness program announced by INS on October 21 and November 13, 1987, Int. Rel. Vol. 64 No. 41, October 26, 1987 at pp. 1191-92, 1200-04; Vol. 64 No. 47, December 14, 1987 at pp. 1368, 1380-81, did not provide for any guarantees for the spouses, children or parents of eligible legalization applicants.

[3]   *Haitian Refugee Center v. Civiletti*, 503 F.Supp. 442 (S.D. Fla. 1980) *affirmed*, 676 F.2d 1023 (5th Cir. Unit B 1982).

[4]   *Orantes-Hernandez v. Smith*, 685 F. Supp. 1488 (C.D. Cal. 1988).

4

State Responsibilities under the Immigration Reform and Control Act of 1986

WALTER BARNES

Chief, Office of Refugee Services, State of California

IRCA imposes some specific responsibilities on States. Two major ones are implementation of the State Legalization Impact Assistance Grant (SLIAG) and the Systematic Alien Verification for Entitlement (SAVE) System.

SLIAG

Under IRCA, Eligible Legalized Aliens (ELA) and Special Agricultural Workers (SAW) and eventually, Replenishment Agricultural Workers (RAW), are eligible for certain Federal and State funded public assistance (PA), public health (PH) and education (Ed) programs. In addition, they are all specifically ineligible for others (*e.g.* - AFDC).[1]

IRCA provides SLIAG funding ($1 Billion a year for four years) to assist states in providing PA, PH and Ed services to ELAs, SAWs and RAWs. To receive such funds, States must file an annual application with the Office of Refugee Resettlement (ORR) and, once approved, comply with required reporting. The funds are not intended to cover all costs associated with delivering services to ELAs, SAWs and RAWs and, therefore, each State must decide how best to utilize the funds available to it.

Most of the major impacted States have developed some form of advisory committee to assist them in developing their SLIAG spending plans. In California, the Health and Welfare Agency (HWA) was designated by the Governor as the lead agency for IRCA implementation and it established a broad-based working advisory group to identify IRCA issues and to provide advice on the State's SLIAG plan. The group is composed of representatives from welfare and immigration rights organizations, organizations assisting aliens through the legalization process, local government, State agencies impacted by IRCA and legislative staff.

Coordination of such a diverse group is difficult but their input has been extremely valuable and, as a result, California completed its proposed SLIAG spending plan in January 1988 and expects to have its SLIAG application into ORR well before the May 15, 1988 due date set by the final SLIAG regulations.

Other States indicate that they too should meet the application due date.

SAVE

Under IRCA, States are required to verify the legal status of all non-citizens applying for federally funded programs. This is to be done through a match with the Immigration and Naturalization Service (INS) data using a system which must be implemented by October 1, 1988. A waiver can be granted, but only when a State can demonstrate that the system will not be cost/beneficial.

The federally funded program for which a match is sought is supposed to pay for 100 percent of the cost of the match even if the person is found to be residing illegally.

Each State must develop procedures and a system to implement the verification process and sign agreements with INS. In California, a subgroup of the advisory group to the HWA has been overseeing the development of SAVE. A recommendation has been made to implement SAVE for PA and PH programs, except Unemployment Insurance (UI) benefits, by using an add-on to the Income Eligibility Verification System (IVES). The subgroup is still working on a recommendation for UI.

A State's ability to meet fully the October 1, 1988 date may be affected by the absence of regulations implementing IRCA provisions, particularly those from the Family Support Administration. However, California is proceeding as though the necessary regulations from all federal agencies will be issued in time for this date to be met.

Other States may be applying for implementation waivers from federal program agencies using the non-cost/benefit argument.

OTHER

States also have interests in assuring that parts of IRCA they are not responsible for are carried out effectively and timely. Three very important examples are:

A. Application for Legalization - States have an interest in assuring that all eligible persons apply for legalization (e.g. - SLIAG funds, continuing problems with illegal population, etc.)

B. Compliance with Legalization Requirements - For the same reasons, States also have an interest in assuring that persons qualifying for temporary residence qualify for permanent status.

C. Public Charge - Confusion of this issue or the wrong decision can mean that applicants may not access services that they need but which would not affect their legalization status. Conversely, they may access services during the temporary residency period that may make them ineligible for permanent residence.

Many states have taken actions to resolve these issues, some in concert with other states or organizations (such as the American Public Welfare Association or the National Governors' Association) and some along. Some examples from California, which we believe are reasonably representative of actions being taken by other States that are impacted by large numbers of ELA and SAW applications, include:

A. California contracted with established and operating legalization services providers to increase the number of applications submitted to INS on behalf of potentially eligible aliens. A total of $1.5 million in State general funds were used for this purpose with a total contract goal of 70,000 increased applications.

B. State agencies are making wage data and other information from State/County files available to applicants to assist them to provide proof of residency to INS.

C. California responded to INS's request for input on A Standardized English language/citizenship test. The proposal is to use the Comprehensive Adult Student Assessment System (CASAS) which is currently used in the Adult Education system in California.

D. California lobbied very hard for a resolution to the concerns raised by INS's initial position on children in foster care.

E. Currently, the State is working on a proposal for a campaign to get information available to applicants and those who have attained temporary residence status to assist them in making an informed choice about whether accessing a particular service might harm their chances for permanent status.

F. The State Employment Agency is assisting employers to meet their employment verification requirements and to ensure that eligible employees are able to obtain jobs to support themselves and their families.

This overview gives you some idea of the activities the States are engaged in in implementing the IRCA provisions. Generally, we believe that it indicates that all States are attempting to conduct themselves in a manner that assures that as many persons as possible will successfully complete the legalization process open to them and eventually become legal citizens.

FOOTNOTES

[1] Two excellent articles on benefits that aliens are eligible for are:
"Aliens' Rights to Public Benefits", Charles Wheeler and Robert Leventhal, *Clearinghouse Review*, December 1988.
"The New Immigration Law: Restrictions on Public Benefits for Amnesty Recipients", National Center for Immigrants' Rights, *Clearinghouse Review*, July 1987.

5

The Implementation of the American Legalization Experiment in Recent Retrospect

GILBERT PAUL CARRASCO [1]

THE United States took a giant step when it provided for the legalization of undocumented immigrants through the enactment of the Immigration Reform and Control Act of 1986. [2] This act signifies not only an opportunity to reduce the number of undocumented persons living in this country by permitting many to obtain legal immigration status, but it has also presented the United States with an opportunity to recast the historical perception of the manner in which it treats immigrants. [3] Unfortunately, the law's implementation has in many respects undermined its overall effectiveness and the equity that Congress intended.

That is not to say, however, that the Immigration and Naturalization Service (I.N.S.) failed to make any effort to create a fair, effective, and reasonable program. To its credit, by the time the application period began on May 5, l987, the I.N.S. has established 107 new legalization offices.

Its attempt to hire courteous staff should also be recognized. Ostensibly, such cognizance of the importance of adjusting the attitudes of the immigration authorities who were ultimately responsible for implementing the program was a lesson learned from the Canadian legalization effect of 1973. [4] Canada's program in this regard gave it substantial credibility with the applicant population and served as an incentive for those eligible to come forward and apply for legalization. [5]

A further assurance included in the American legalization statute was a provision authorizing "Qualified Designated Entities" (QDEs to serve as filing sites in addition to the offices of the Attorney General. [6] These QDEs were intended [7] to serve as the buffer between the Government and the undocumented. Hundreds of non-profit organizations were authorized by I.N.S. to provide counsel and assistance to those reluctant to trust the system and to would-be applicants who were simple befuddled by the maze of technical detail that is characteristic of the law.

Although it is likely that most of the three million applicants for legalization received assistance from the QDE before submitting an application (in addition to perhaps millions who never applied), many applicants ultimately did not file through QDEs because of the I.N.S.' interpretation of the statute with respect to employment authorization. Upon filing a prima facie application, the statute provides that an applicant shall receive work authorization. [8] Of course, with the advent of employer sanctions making it unlawful to hire the undocumented, [9] such permission to work took on great significance, particularly in the hiatus between submission of the application and its adjudication.

The Qualified Designated Entities, however, were not permitted to transit employment authorization even though they were statutorily authorized to receive applications. Such extension of temporary work authorization would not have constituted "a final determination on the application" which of course, had to be made by the Attorney General. [10] Because of the need to obtain permission to work expeditiously, many applicants, therefore, went directly to the I.N.S. to apply.

The National Coordinating Agency Qualified Designated Entities attempted to persuade the I.N.S. that temporary employment authorization could attend the filing of an application with a QDE. However, the I.N.S. persisted in its position that such a policy would involve QDEs in the adjudication of applications.

Nevertheless, the Qualified Designated Entities undertook a monumental effort in the legalization process, establishing professional training regimens, efficient processing systems, extensive pro bono networks, and sophisticated computer programs for the yearlong program. Indeed, over 500,000 applicants officially filed their applications through QDEs, fully 17.1 percent of the total. [11] Although the I.N.S. support of the QDEs in the process was uneven, these organizations made a substantial contribution to the success of this American experiment.

The Immigration and Naturalization Service is also to be commended for its adoption of a dialogistic regulatory process. Its release of a preliminary working draft of the legalization regulations in the late 1986 was particularly appropriate given the unprecedented nature of the new law. The dispatch with which the draft regulations were issued, unfortunately, was not maintained thereafter. Proposed regulations were published in the Federal Register in March 1987, and final regulations were not issued until May 1, 1987, just four days before the commencement of the application period. The delays in the promulgation of regulations caused difficulty for practitioner and applicant alike, simply from the standpoint of ascertaining what the governing law was. What was most unfortunate, however, was the apparent disregard of voluminous comments to the regulations submitted by attorneys and organizations from all over the country. Ironically, many of those same comments were ultimately by I.N.S. in the form of "legalization wires" issued at various times during the application period, purportedly superseding previously promulgated regulations.

The issue of "family fairness" indubitably played a part in limiting the number of applications that were submitted. Specifically, the lack of protection for ineligible spouses and exposure of them to deportation was not required by statute and could have been obviated through a more humanitarian response to the problem. If the Attorney General had used his discretion to accord such individuals deferred action status, for example, it may very well have resulted in significantly more applications. [12]

The issue of cost has a greater prominence than is generally recognized. The application fee of $185.00 was used to cover implementation of the entire program (i.e., staffing, facilities, etc.). This cost was simply prohibitive for many families in the eligible population, particularly when it is considered that the additional cost of waivers, medical examinations, fingerprints, photographs, and legal fees was also commonly necessary. A typical family of four likely faced expenses of upward of $1,000. [13] Underscoring this difficulty are the 1986 census data indicating that the median household income of Hispanics of Mexican origin was $19,326. [14] As expected, most applicants for legalization were Mexican nationals. [15] It is, indeed, unfortunate that some of those who were eligible for legalization simply could not afford to apply.

Illustrative of the interpretive approach of the I.N.S. disfavoring eligibility is the controversy with respect to the meaning of "unlawful status known to the Government." [16] Particularly at the earlier stages of implementation, rigid regulatory interpretation of statutory provisions by the I.N.S. led to confusion and litigation that could have been obviated. In retrospect, the Government's implementation effort was hampered by such a restrictive perspective more than by any other single factor. This perspective was contrary to the explicit legislative intent "that the legalization program should be implemented in a liberal and generous fashion, as has been historical pattern with other forms of administrative relief granted by Congress." [17]

The controversy involved the statutory provision entitling nonimmigrants whose unlawful status was known to the Government as of January 1, 1982 to qualify for legalization. In both the preliminary working draft regulations and in the proposed regulations the I.N.S. limited the term 'Government' to mean 'I.N.S.' [18] Despite I.N.S.' own admission that of 91 comments received on the issue, "all of the comments clearly stated that the definition was far too restrictive and should be modified to include all Federal agencies," [19] the regulation was promulgated in final form retaining the same illegitimate definition. [20] It took months of litigation and the Orders of two federal district courts for I.N.S. finally to accede to the proper and plain interpretation of the law. [21]

CONCLUSION

All things considered, the American legalization experiment was generally a success, given its statutory parameters. Nevertheless, it is apparent that there is a sound basis for the conclusion that there are substantially more people who were ineligible and who remain in undocumented status than there are those who were eligible. [22]

This result is due more to the statutory framework than to deficiencies in implementation. Although the law was based on the Immigration and Refugee Policy, [23] the implicit recommendation regarding duration of residency was, unfortunately, not accorded its necessary importance. When the Commission issued its report in March 1981, its recommendation was that applicants must have resided in the United States continuously since January 1, 1980, a period of little more than one year.

Regrettably, the successive Congress that considered predecessor versions of what was ultimately enacted into law in the form of the Immigration Reform and Control Act of 1986 did not take care to advance the eligibility date when the bills were reconsidered after failing to pass in the preceding Congresses. Indeed the Senate retained in the 1980 eligibility date in the Simpson-Rodino Bill until it receded to the House in conference with respect to that provision. [24] Alas, the House version with its 1982 date was still far from adequate to "wipe the slate clean" in accord with the statutory intent as embodied in the legislative history.

EPILOGUE

If it is the desire of Congress to resolve the plight of this shadow population, a population now more vulnerable to exploitation and abuse when ever (in light of employer sanctions), it will be simply be necessary, as difficult as it may be, to legislate a second legalization. If this nation is truly bound to the idea of starting with a clean slate, a relatively current eligibility date regarding residence is quintessential to that worthy objective.

FOOTNOTES

[1]   Gilbert Paul Carrasco is a visiting professor of law at Seton Hall University School of Law in Newark, New Jersey. At the time this presentation was delivered during the proceedings of the 1988 National Legal Conference on Immigration and Refugee Policy, Professor Carrasco was Director of Immigration Services for the national office of the United States Catholic Conference in Washington, D. C. The assistance of Iryna H. Lomaga and Michael Kestan, student research assistants, at Seton Hall Law School is hereby gratefully acknowledged.

[2]   Immigration Reform and Control Act of 1986, Pub. L. No. 99-603, 100 Stat. 3359 (codified in scattered sections of 8 U.S.C.).

[3]   Carrasco, "The Golden Moment of Legalization," In Defense of the Alien 32 (1988).

[4]   Canadian Statutes, 1974 Rev., Chap. 27, Section 8, p. 429.

5   Meissner, Papademetriou, and North, *Legalization of Undocumented Aliens: Lessons From Other Countries* at 14 (1987); *see also, Library of Congress, Congressional Research Service, Education and Public Welfare Division,* prepared for *House Comm. on the Judiciary,* 99th Cong., lst Sess., *Impact of Illegal Immigration and Background on Legalization: Programs of Other Countries* 147-52 (Comm. Print 1985).

6   "The Attorney General shall provide that applications for adjustment of status under subsection (a) of this section may be filed - (A) with the Attorney General, or (B) with a Qualfied Designated Entity, but only if the applicant consents·to the forwarding of the application to the Attorney General." Immigration Reform and Control Act of 1986, Section 245(c) (1), 8 U.S.C. Section 1255 (c) (1) (West Supp. 1987); as applied to Special Agricultural Workers, *see* Section 2120 (b) (1), 8 U.S.C. Section 1160(b) (1) (West Supp. 1987).

7   H.R. Rep. No. 99-682, Part 1, 99th Cong., 2d Sess. 73 (1986).

8   "The Attorney General shall provide that in the case of an alien who presents a prima facie application for adjustment status under subsection (2) during the application period, and until a final determination on the application has been made in accordance with this section, the alien - (A) may not be deported, and (B) shall be granted authorization to engage in employment in the United States and be provided an "employment authorized" endorsement or other appropriate work permit." Section 245 (A) (e) (2), 8 U.S.C. Section 1225(e) (2) (West Supp. 1987); *cf.,* Section 210 (a) (d) (2), 8 U.S.C. Section 1160 (d) (West Supp. 1987) (Special Agricultural Workers who present a "nonfrivolous application").

9   Section 274A, 8 U.S.A. Section 1324a (West Supp. 1987).

10   *Supra,* n. 7; *but see* Section 245A (c) (3), 8 U.S.C. Section 1255a(c) (3) (West Supp. 1987) *and* Section 210(b) (4), 8 U.S.C. Section 1160(b) (4) (West Supp. 1987).

11   This figure represents data received as of December 14, l988 by telephone from Raymond Penn, I.N.S. Assistant Commissioner for Legalization. The QDEs have submitted 507,632 of a total of 2,961.048 applications. Remaining Special Agricultural Worker applications filed with QDEs will have been forwarded to the I.N.S. by January 30, l989.

12   See Sanger, "Immigration Reform and Control of the Undocumented Family," 2 *Geo. Imm. L.J.* 295, 298 (1987); *Review of the Early Implementation of the Immigration Reform and Control Act of 1986: Hearing Before the Subcomm. on Immigration and Refugee Affairs of the Senate Comm. on the Judiciary,* 100th Cong., lst Sess. 5-10 (1987) (statement of Rev. Msgr. Nicholas DiMarzio, U.S. Catholic Conference).

13   *See I.N.S. and the Budgetary Impact of Implementing the Immigration Reform and Control Act of 1986: Hearing Before the House Comm. on the Budget,* 100th Cong., 1st Sess. 22, 50 (statement of Gilbert Paul Carrasco, Director of Immigration Services, United States Conference).

14   1980 Census of Population and Housing; Provisional Estimates of Social, Economic, and Housing Characteristics (Revis'd Est. 1986).

15   In Texas, for example, 87 percent of the applicants were Mexican nationals. California's data show that 81 percent of the applicants were Mexican. In some places, the applicants were nearly all of Mexican origin (*e.g.,* Oregon 95.5 percent). Refugee Policy Group, *Serving the Newly Legalized: Their Characteristics and Needs,* 12 (June 198).

16   Section 245A(a) (2) (B), 8 U.S.C. Section 1255a(a) (2) (B) (West Supp. 1987).

17   H.R. Rep. No. 99-682 (I) 72 (1986).

18   *See* 52 Fed. Reg. at 8752 (March 19, l987).

19   52 Fed. Reg. at 16202 (May l, 1987).

20   52 Fed. Reg. at 16206 (May l, l987) [*codified at* 8 C.F.R. Section 243a.l (d)].

[21]   *Farzad v. Chandler*, 670 F.Supp. 690 (N.D. Tex. 1987); *Ayuda, Inc. v. Meese*, 687 F.Supp. 650 (D.D.C. 1988). The author is counsel of record in *Ayuda*. The issue as to whether the applicants can receive any benefits under the law if they did not apply by the end of the application period is still being litigated. *Ayuda, Inc. v. Meese*, No. 88-5226 (D.C. Cir.) (oral argument scheduled for March 7, 1989); *see also In re Richard Thornburgh*, No. 88-5360 (D.C. Cir.) (petition for mandamus pending).

[22]   Meissner & Papademetriou, *The Legalization Countdown: A Third Quarter Assessment* (1988) (Report of the Carnegie Endowment for International Peace).

[23]   Submitted to Congress and the President pursuant to Pub. L. 95-412.

[24]   *House Conference Report* No. 99-1000, 99th Cong., 2d Sess. 92 (1986).

PART II

EMPLOYER SANCTIONS AND DISCRIMINATION

6

Immigration Reform: Status of Implementing Employer Sanctions After One Year

ARNOLD P. JONES
Senior Associate Director, U.S. General Accounting Office

DURING the past fifteen years, Congress has been increasingly concerned that aliens not authorized to work were taking jobs away from authorized workers and adversely affecting the U.S. economy. Federal law, however, did not prohibit or provide penalties for employers who knowingly hired unauthorized aliens. GAO reported in 1985 that most countries that had enacted laws penalizing employers of unauthorized aliens believed that these sanctions were a deterrent to unauthorized alien employment.

On November 6, 1986, the Immigration Reform and Control Act of 1986 became law. This law: 1) contains civil and criminal penalties for employers of unauthorized aliens; and 2) requires all employers in the nation to complete an employment eligibilty verification form (I-9) for each new employee.

Because of concern that employers, to avoid being sanctioned, would not hire 'foreign-looking' U.S. citizens or legal aliens, Congress added a provision to the law that prohibits employers with four or more employees from discriminating on the basis of a person's national origin or citizenship status. This provision expanded the percentage of the nation's employers who could be charged with discrimination under federal law from about thirteen to 48 percent. Employers who violate this provision can be fined.

The law and implementing regulations establish timetables for enforcement and related penalties. The implementation has three phases: a 6-month education period; a 1-year period during which warnings will be issued to first-time violators; and full enforcement of sanctions without a warning against those who violate the law.

The law requires that each of GAO's annual reports reviews the implementation and enforcement of the employer sanctions law for the purpose of determining whether: 1) the law has been carried out satisfactorily; 2) a pattern of discrimination has resulted against authorized workers; and 3) an unnecessary regulatory burden has been created for employers. GAO will also attempt to determine if the anti-discrimination provision creates an unreasonable burden for employers.

The law states that Congress may use expedited procedures to repeal both the employer sanction and anti-discrimination provisions if GAO's third annual report finds a "widespread pattern" of discrimination caused "solely" by the sanctions provision. If GAO's third annual report finds "no significant discrimination," or alternatively finds an unreasonable burden for employers, the law provides expedited procedures for Congress to repeal the anti-discrimination provision.

In GAO's opinion, the general approach followed during the first year to implement the law has been satisfactory. So far, the data on discrimination related to the law has not shown a pattern of discrimination or unreasonable burden on employers. However, because of the many factors involved, GAO may not be able to isolate and measure the effects of employer sanctions on any identified discrimination. Insufficient data exist for GAO to determine if the Act's regulatory burden on employers is unnecessary and it is unlikely such data will be available.

EDUCATIONAL PHASE

INS efforts to implement the law have primarily focused on educating the public about the law to help assure voluntary compliance. Handbooks explaining the law have been mailed to the nation's estimated seven million employers and INS has begun a national media campaign to educate the public.

PLANNED ENFORCEMENT

INS plans to allocate about $60 million during fiscal year 1988 to implement the law's employer sanctions provision. With this amount, INS plans to target about 20,000 employers for compliance investigations. In addition, Department of Labor employees, who visit 60,000 employers annually to enforce various labor laws, began on September 1, 1987, to also inspect employers' I-9 forms for compliance. As of October 7, 1987, two employers have been served notice under the law for knowingly hiring unauthorized aliens.

PATTERN OF DISCRIMINATION

As of September 1987, 67 alleged employer violations of the law's anti-discrimination provisions have been filed with federal agencies — 44 are in process and 23 were closed.

The Equal Opportunity Commission — the agency that administers title VII of the Civil Rights Act of 1964 prohibiting national origin discrimination — had received 52 charges related to employer sanctions. Most of these charges were still in process as of September 1987.

The Office of Special Counsel in the Department of Justice — responsible under the law for prosecuting discrimination charges had received 15 charges related to employer sanctions. Two have been dismissed, one withdrawn, and the rest are under investigation. An additional 34 charges have been filed with four state and local government agencies.

The discrimination charges under investigation do not, in GAO's opinion, constitute: 1) a pattern of discrimination; or 2) an unreasonable regulatory burden for employers. INS has just begun to enforce the law's sanction provision. Thus, until now, employers have had little reason not to hire "foreign-looking" citizens or legal aliens to avoid being sanctioned.

Once full enforcement begins, GAO may still not be able to determine if any discrimination that does occur is caused "solely" by employers' fear of sanctions. Various federal officials with experience in discrimination cases said that normally judges' decisions in cases of discrimination do not specify what caused the discriminatory act. Furthermore, no data exist on the number of persons who applied for the estimated 67.5 million jobs filled each year who are not hired because of employers' fear of sanctions. Without this information, it may not be possible for GAO to determine what is a "widespread pattern" of discrimination versus "no significant" discrimination.

DATA LIMITATIONS

GAO believes that the ultimate test of whether the burden imposed on employers is worth the cost involved is the extent to which these activities are accompanied by and contribute to desired reductions in unauthorized alien employment and illegal immigration. Unfortunately, it will be extremely difficult, if not impossible, to conclusively establish such a cause/effect relationship. Further, even if no progress is realized, the employer requirements may still be a necessary part of a revised strategy.

GAO has selected three indicators of the law's effect on illegal immigration and will use these and other data in its subsequent annual reports. Although these indicators are the best available, they are difficult to measure and may be influenced by many factors other than employer sanctions. Therefore, it is likely that the results of GAO's future analysis of the law's effect on illegal immigration may be inconclusive.

Based on public comments, INS revised its regulations to reduce the burden on employers and placement agencies who recruit or refer job applicants to employers for a fee.

In addition, in November 1987, GAO sent a questionnaire on the new law to 6,000 randomly selected employers nationwide. The results will be available in our second annual report.

From my remarks, you can tell that we have reservations about our ability to answer the mandated questions and about the availability of data. If you have any suggestions or thoughts regarding our approach or sources for data please call James Blume of my staff on (202) 357-1007, so that we can consider your ideas in our second and third reports.

7

The Office of Special Counsel for Immigration Related Unfair Employment. Practices of the U.S. Department of Justice

LAWRENCE J. SISKIND
Special Counsel for Immigration Related Unfair Employment Practices, U.S. Dept. of Justice

THE office for Immigration Related Unfair Employment Practices was created by the Immigration Reform and Control Act of 1986 (IRCA) to enforce the ban against national origin and citizenship status employment discrimination. The Office of Special Counsel, in which I serve, is an independent unit within the Department of Justice.

Our work focuses on three major activities: 1) education; 2) litigation; and 3) independent investigation.

First, education. Since we are a new office, enforcing a new law, education was our top job during our first year, and continues to be a high priority during our second. Office of Special Counsel attorneys have given over 70 presentations at seminars, conferences, and meetings throughout the country. We have spoken to employer groups, unions, attorneys, personnel officers, public interest groups, and federal agencies, including the Immigration and Naturalization Service (INS), U.S. Attorneys' offices, and the Equal Employment Opportunity Commission (EEOC). We participated in the preparation of a number of videotapes and videotaped programs to help educate attorneys and the general public about the new immigration law.

We have responded to over 1700 telephone and written requests for information. The Office has a toll free telephone line (1-800-255-7688) to make it more accessible to individuals outside the Washington, D.C. area. We also have two local numbers, one with a TDD device for the hearing impaired. Our TDD number is 202-653-5710. Our other local number is 202-653-8121. For after hours, a recording in both Spanish and English informs callers that if they leave a message it will be responded to as soon as possible. No one who calls or writes my Office for informaton is ignored. Everyone gets a response.

We have distributed several thousand informational packets containing charge forms, in both Spanish and English, and explanatory material concerning IRCA's nondiscrimination provision. These packets have been sent to every U.S. Attorneys' office, every EEOC district office, every INS district office, every Qualified Designated Entity ("QDEs" are organizations established under IRCA to help aliens avail themselves of the Act's amnesty program), and numerous public interest organizations and state and local civil rights agencies.

Our Office has been working in conjunction with the INS to produce a handbook entitled *The New Immigration Law - Your Rights and Your Job*, which sets out employee rights under IRCA's antidiscrimination provision. Publication of the employee rights handbook is in the final stages; close to 500,000 handbooks will be distributed. This handbook will complement the already issued *Handbook for Employers - Instructions for Completing Form I-9*, which includes information on the nondiscrimination provision and contacting the Office. Over seven million employer handbooks have been distributed.

We are about to start a campaign of public service advertisements, in Spanish and English, on radio and television stations across the country. I am pleased to report that Jimmy Smits, star of the LA Law television program, has agreed to donate his services for this campaign.

The second focus of our work is litigation. We process charges of national origin and citizens and state and local civil rights aged, we help claimants fill them out. Once they're complete, we investigate. After 120 days, we determine whether or not to file complaints based on the charges.

As of this morning, my Office has received 105 charges: 99 against private employers, one against an association, one against a federal agency, one against a state agency, one against a public school district, one against a city, and one against a union. Of these charges, 47 are complete and under investigation, 23 are incomplete with requests for additional information outstanding, and four voluntarily withdrawn after the injured parties were rehired with backpay. We've dismissed 27 charges either because the injured party never provided enough information to render the charge complete, or because we found no reasonable cause to believe that discrimination had occurred.

About seventy percent of the charges are from New York, California and Texas. About half of the charges are brought to us by public interest organizations, law firms, and unions. The rest come direct from the injured parties.

I pass these statistics on with a caveat. I would not advise drawing conclusions from them anymore than I would advise predicting the next President on the basis of the Iowa caucuses. This is a small and non-representative universe. For example, nine charges — about ten percent of all our charges — come from the same woman from a large Northeast city. Employer sanctions, which many expect will be the driving force generating these charges, are still in the early stages of enforcement. Random audits by the INS of employers have just begun. In June, the INS plans to begin issuing fines for first violations. Presently they visit employers at least twice before issuing fines. So the numbers may hold some interest, but at this stage I don't consider them very important.

Our third focus is independent investigations. I really want to stress this one. We don't wait for others to come to us with charges. Our job is to combat discrimination whenever and wherever we find it.

Right now we have over 300 independent investigations at various stages of progress. Over 70 companies representing several hundred thousand job opportunities have already agreed to change their hiring practices because of our intervention. If our investigations uncover illegal activity, and if the affected entities refuse to change their practices, we may file independent complaints.

So far, we have not found a strong correlation between discrimination and employer sanctions. In each of the complaints we've filed, and in each of the matters we've settled, the discrimination was the result of policies which were in place before IRCA became law. On the other hand, several charges under investigation involve discriminatory acts which occurred in the spring and summer of 1987, around the time employer sanctions first went into effect. It is very possible that our investigations will turn up evidence linking the discriminatory acts to fear of employer sanctions. As I mentioned earlier, enforcement of employer sanctions is still in the preliminary stages. So from our vantage point, the jury is still out on the question of whether employer sanctions cause discrimination.

This Committee should recognize that our findings on this issue are of limited value. We do not see all charges of discrimination. First, our jurisdiction is limited. On national origin discrimination, for example, our jurisdiction is limited to cases involving employers with four to fourteen employees. It is theoretically possible that large employers, fearful of sanctions, could be engaging in significant national origin discrimination without any charges being filed with our Office.

Second, our investigations don't focus on motive. They focus on intent. There's an important difference. We go after employers who knowingly and intentionally discriminate. It doesn't matter to us *why* they discriminate. If the discrimination is intentional — rather than accidental or coincidental — we will prosecute. Motive may be relevant to intent but it is not dispositive. Therefore we may deal with employers who are motivated by fear of sanctions without our ever discovering that fact. All we have to prove to win our case in court is that the employer intended to do what it did. We don't have to prove why it did it.

I want to say a final word about the approach we bring to our job. We at the Office of Special Counsel never forget that we're lawyers and that our clients are the people of the United States of America. The people, through Congress, have decided that discrimination in employment on the basis of national origin and citizenship status is wrong and should be prohibited. Our job, as good lawyers, is to faithfully and zealously advance our clients' will.

8

The Immigration and Naturalization Service and Employer Sanctions Provisions

JOHN F. SHAW
INS Assistant Commissioner for Investigations

WHEN the Immigration Reform and Control Act was passed, in November of 1986, it marked the culmination of years of effort to create a fair and balanced reform of U.S. immigration laws. This law established a legalization program permitting persons who had resided in our nation continuously, but unlawfully, since prior to January 1982 to obtain legal status. Under this program, more than one million persons have come forward to apply for legalization — more than any other amnesty program established in the world — and the Service is continuing to reach out to eligible persons and encouraging them to apply.

The one-time legalization opportunity is balanced with the employer sanctions provisions, which make it unlawful to hire persons who are not eligible for employment in the United States. The Service saw sanctions as a critical element in reinforcing our nation's system of legal immigration. The sanctions provisions are carefully balanced with protections for both the employer and the employee.

The protection for employers is contained in the verification requirements of the Act. The substantive provisions apply to "knowing" violations of the law — for instance, to employers who hire unauthorized aliens knowing that they lack employment authorization. The law affords employers a means of establishing knowledge of their employees' status by requiring them to complete the employment eligibility verification process, including a review of employees' identity and employment eligibility documents and completion of the I-9 Form. Employers who follow all steps in the verification process are entitled to raise a rebuttable "good faith" defense with respect to the substantive provisions of the law.

The verification system also protects employees against discrimination. First, the system provides citizens and authorized workers of all races and national backgrounds with a means of establishing their eligibility to work.

Second, the verification requirements are mandatory for all employees hired after the law took effect. As a result, although there were fears before the law was passed that employers might be reluctant to hire persons who "looked" or "sounded" foreign, the verification system addressed that concern by requiring like treatment for all eligible workers, regardless of their citizenship status, race, or national origin.

To further protect employees, the law created a new cause of action prohibiting employment discrimination against any individual, other than an unauthorized alien, on the basis of national origin or, in the case of a citizen or intending citizen, on the basis of citizenship status. The Act also established a special administrative process for prosecuting claims. Prosecution of those claims is handled by an independent office within the Department of Justice, the Office of Special Counsel for Immigration-Related Unfair Employment Practices. In creating this distinct dichotomy of accountability between the agency responsible for enforcement of employer sanctons (the Office of Special Counsel), Congress has ensured that neither a conflict of interest nor the appearance of a conflict of interest will arise in the implementation of the statutory scheme.

Nonetheless, we at the Service recognize our responsibility, both as members of the federal community and as individual members of society, in working with the Office of Special Counsel, the Equal Employment Opportunity Commission, and other agencies to allay the understandable fears, which many minority members of our communities may hold, that the new law may have a discriminatory impact on them. I believe that our first year of implementation went far toward accomplishing this goal, and, in so doing, furthered the overall goals of the immigration reform law.

Following, is a brief review of some of the steps we have taken as a part of our responsibility to implement the sanctions provisions in a manner which advances the goal of ensuring the fair treatment of all eligible workers. As I noted, Congress took the first step toward that goal by mandating the applicability of the verification scheme to all persons — even Congress itself is not exempt from those requirements which, as many are aware, cannot be said of all legislation of this kind. For instance, Congress specifically exempted itself from compliance with the equal employment opportunity laws of the United States.

In developing its implementing regulations, the Service reinforced equal treatment with a number of key provisions. We have also attempted to adopt a flexible, common-sense approach to verification, which permits a variety of identity and employment eligibility documents while at the same time minimizing the possibility of fraud. We especially attempted to be flexible in the requirements for minors, recognizing that many underprivileged youths, who particularly need and desire employment, might not possess or be able to afford the fee to obtain some identity documents such as a driver's license. In a series of technical amendments to these regulations, the Service now also permits the same verification procedures for sixteen and seventeen year-olds and the mentally or physically disabled.

The Service has also recognized the potential of certain portions of the sanctions provisions as tools to promote the hiring of the disadvantaged and under-employed. I am making specific reference to the section of the law that permits State employment service agencies to conduct the verification process on behalf of employers. The Service has developed regulations which encourage employers to take advantage of this provision and use such agencies, which have traditionally shown themselves to be effective in the referral and placement of disadvantaged and minority workers who frequently cannot afford the fees charged by job placement services in the private sector.

In furtherance of this concept, the Service is also reaching out to a variety of agencies and service organizations through its Legally Authorized Worker, or LAW, program. As envisioned by the Service, as sanctions create more job opportunities for the eligible workforce, these efforts will aid employers in identifying sources of legal employees, among both the native, and immigrant and refugee, populations of the United States..

To ensure that employers are aware of and understand their responsibilities under the new law, the Service has embarked on an unprecedented educational effort. The Service prepared and disseminated more than eight and one-half million copies of a comprehensive *Handbook for Employers*, which includes a discussion of the anti-discrimination provisions and the duties of the Office of Special Counsel. The *Handbook* has been distributed through a variety of means, including direct mail, the Small Business Administration, the Department of Labor, and all INS field offices.

The Service also has an ongoing program of seminars for, and personal contacts with, employers. One-to-one educational visits have been made with more than one-half million employers nationwide. These personal contacts also provide employers with guidance how to comply with the law while avoiding the prohibited employment-related discrimination practices, a topic covered in depth in the field manual provided to all Service enforcement officers. We are pleased with the level of cooperation and assistance which has been provided to us by the Office of Special Counsel in the preparation of our educational materials.

The Service has also maintained a progressive public relations campaign consisting of media saturation in local newspapers, and radio and television stations, in major metropolitan areas throughout the United States. This campaign has sought to provide an element of balance to our expectations of employer compliance combined with necessary enforcement efforts against willful violators, and public understanding of an employee's rights to fair and equitable treatment.

From the start, the Service has believed that an aggressive educational program lays the foundation for successful implementation of the sanctions laws, by creating a climate of voluntary compliance for all employers. That this result has been achieved is evident from the assessments of diverse objective observers that sanctions are "working". Most significantly, our hundreds of thousands of contacts with employers have revealed widespread compliance with and support for the law.

This conclusion is supported by a recent assessment by Representative Charles Schumer, Democrat of New York, who has been a watchful observer of the efforts of the Immigration Service in all aspects of our implementation of the reform law. Congressman Schumer issued a report concluding that:

1. Sanctions are working;
2. Sanctions have not been overly burdensome to business;
3. Sanctions have not caused massive disruptions in the labor market; and
4. Sanctions have not resulted in discrimination.

The same conclusion is supported by the results of a survey conducted in August by the Chamber of Commerce. In that survey of over 22,000 employers, the Chamber found that:

- 92 percent were aware of their obligations under the immigration reform law;

- 85 percent indicated that they intended to comply with the law, 57 percent of whom indicated that they were already in full compliance; and

- 40 percent found the law easy to comply with; it is significant that many other employers indicated that they had changed their hiring procedures or sought outside counsel — another indicator of the level of compliance and, we believe, one that suggests hieghtened awareness of their concurrent responsibilities to perform the verification procedures equitably.

To monitor the impact of the new law, Congress required that the General Accounting Office (GAO) provide three annual reports reviewing the implementation and enforcement of employer sanctions to determine the following: 1) whether sanctions have been implemented satisfactorily; 2) whether a pattern of discrimination against citizens, nationals, or other eligible workers has resulted; and 3) whether sanctions created an unnecessary regulatory burden for employers. The first of these reports was issued in early November, and was highly favorable. In particular, GAO made the following statement:

> In GAO's opinion, the general approach followed during the first year to implement the law has been satisfactory. So far, the data on discrimination related to the law has not shown a pattern of discrimination or unreasonable burden on employers ...INS's overall strategy...is reasonable. As a result, we believe that pro-

gress made during the first year to implement the law is satisfactory.

In conclusion, the Immigration and Naturalization Service is committed to implementing the law in a fair and equitable manner, and we believe that this is evident from all perspectives.

PART III

BEYOND IRCA: CURRENT LEGISLATIVE INITIATIVES

9

Beyond IRCA: Legal Immigration and the National Interest

LAWRENCE H. FUCHS
Mayer and Walter Jaffe Professor of American Civilization and Politics
Brandeis University

THIS presentation examines the legislative initiative involved in S. 2104, which passed the United States Senate on March 15, 1988, by a vote of eighty-eight to four, in the light of the recommendations of the Select Commission on Immigration and Refugee Policy concerning legal immigration. Although the issue of illegal immigration occupied highest priority with the Select Commission, there were actually more specific recommendations made by the Commission on legal immigration (twenty) than illegal immigration (fifteen) among the total of one hundred and seven recommendations made on all aspects of immigration and refugee policy in its report submitted to the President and the Congress in March 1981.

PREMISES UNDERLYING RECOMMENDATIONS OF SCIRP CONCERNING LEGAL IMMIGRATION

One premise that underlay the work of the Commission was that the effective curtailment of illegal immigration was tied to changes in the law regarding legal immigration (including the legalization program). For example, it was widely believed that the entire system of legal immigration was, to some extent, jeopardized by the continued growth in illegal immigration. It was also widely believed on the Commission that changes in the immigration law regarding legal immigration might help to inhibit illegal migration pressures.

In addition to these premises, the Commission approached questions dealing with the lawful admission of immigrants on the basis of two other premises which were so widely assumed that they hardly ever were discussed: first, that whatever was done to change our system of lawful admissions, the old system of allocating visas on the basis of national origins was dead; and second, that whatever was done to change our system of lawful immigration, family reunification would remain the basis for allocating visas. In all my discussions with sixteen Commissioners, I never once heard these assumptions challenged.

THE FUNDAMENTAL ISSUE

But that still left room for a great deal of discussion as to what changes in our lawful admission system would be desirable. The obvious questions on almost everyone's mind were: About how many immigrants should be admitted each year? Should the total number of immigrants be capped? Should the balance between non-family related immigrants and family reunification immigrants be altered? And if so, in what ways? Should changes be made within and among the family reunification categories? What changes, if any, should be made in the categories of non-family or independent immigrants and in the methods used in choosing them?

These questions were subject to intense discussion among Commissioners early in their deliberations following the submission to them by the staff of a model for a new immigration system which, for the sake of stimulating that discussion, proposed immigration at an annual level of 750,000, capped at that figure, including the immediate relative of U.S. citizens and refugees. The model provided for three fundamentally separate immigration tracks based on specified goals of immigration policy: family reunification; independent immigrants; and refugees.

A large majority of the Commissioners reacted negatively to the ideal of an overall cap. Eventually, when the Commissioners voted on that issue on December 6, 1980, they voted fifteen to one against a cap on the total number of immigrants and refugees and for the retention of a system where some immigrants are numerically limited but others -- such as spouses, children and parents of U.S. citizens and refugees -- are exempt from any ceilings or targets. Only Senator Alan Simpson (R-Wyoming) expressed the view that "there should be a firm cap"

Commissioners were invited to propose their own models to see how much common ground could be found on the basic questions of legal immigration. Among the several that were submitted, not one proposed a cutback in the total number of immigrants then being admitted to the United States. The high number was up to one million, suggested by Attorney General Benjamin Civiletti; the low number was 550,000 to 650,000 subject to a firm cap, as proposed by Senator Simpson.

From an historian's point of view, the most interesting thing about the discussion on numbers was that not one Commissioner proposed a cutback. When one considers that at that very time the United States economy was experiencing a sharp downturn while the apprehension of illegal aliens was climbing quickly and that most of the discussion took place soon after the Mariel boatlift, the generally positive view which the Commissioners had toward lawful immigration put them in sharp contrast to the Dillingham Commission of 1909-1911.

The discussion on numbers was all the more remarkable because most of the results of research on the impact of lawful immigration commissioned by SCIRP was not yet available. When the Commissioners made their final recommendations, they and their staffs had available to them the full research reports or condensations of research on impacts of recent immigration and questions concerning their acculturation. The general conclusion was that lawful immigration, while it created some problems of competition and friction with U.S. citizens (and certainly of perceived competition), was generally good for the United States.

The research results suggested that, compared to other times, the most recent immigrants were disproportionately educated and skilled. They adapted relatively well economically and also socially, perhaps partly because they met all the tests of exclusion and also arrived in the United States to be met by close family members. It showed that immigrants were efficient taxpayers, tended to be healthy, and that overall their children did better in schools and were healthier than the children of native born Americans (that was especially true for Asians). These conclusions, which were available to the Commissioners when they made their final recommendations, have been confirmed repeatedly by research since 1981.

THE QUESTION OF A CAP

Perhaps of even greater importance than research with respect to the question of restricting immigration numbers was the fact that ninety percent of all immigrants admitted lawfully to the United States came on the basis of family reunification, signifying that there would be a political cost for a great many high appointed or elected officials should they champion the cause of overall restriction. Yet, Senator Walter Huddleston (D-Kentucky) managed in 1980 to obtain the signatures of about one third of the Senate to a proposal to cap the total number of immigrants (including refugees) at 350,000, undoubtedly a reaction in part to the growing unease in the country about immigration — legal and illegal, and refugee flows — at a time of economic uncertainty.

The clear signal from a large majority of Commissioners to the staff was that they did not want a cap and that they were comfortable with an overall admissions number of at least 550,000 not counting refugees, provided something could be done to curtail illegal migration to the United States.

Working on the assumption that reasonably effective measures would be taken to reduce the number of illegal aliens entering and remaining in the United States, the Commission explored the question of immigration categories within the framework of a discussion of immigration goals, which formed the basis for the recommendations on lawful admissions.

IMMIGRATION GOALS AND IMMIGRATION TRACKS

The Commission had no difficulty in establishing the three goals of immigration policy: family reunification; independent immigration for the explicit purpose of strengthening American society; and refugee admissions for the United States to take its fair share of refugees, a goal that was quickly met by the passage of the Refugee Act of 1980, which the Commission unanimously endorsed in its final recommendations, while making certain suggestions to improve its implementation.

The first two goals of immigration were reflected in the immigration admissions system proposed by the Commission. For the first time in the history of U.S. immigration policy, it was proposed that family reunification immigrants and non-family or independent immigrants be admitted through separate visa allocation systems in which the two types of immigrants would not compete with one another for the same visas (The vote was sixteen to zero for separate systems).

EXEMPTIONS FOR IMMEDIATE RELATIVES OF U.S. CITIZENS VS. THE CAP

S. 2104 embodies three important recommendations made by the Select Commission, but it differs from those recommendations in several other respects. It follows the Select Commission recommendations in creating separate tracks for immigrants who are family related and those who are not (who come independently). It also calls for an increase in the the absolute number of immigrants admitted lawfully and for an expansion in the number of immigrants admitted independent of family reunification, slightly tipping the ratio of independent to family related immigrants.

Like the Select Commission, it repudiates the notion that refugees should be admitted in competition with either family related or independent immigrants.

In other respects, S. 2104 does not reflect the confidence in immigration which is embodied in the recommendations of the Select Commission. As already mentioned, the Select Commision voted overwhelmingly against a cap. S. 2104 caps immigration at 590,000, except for refugees, who could still adjust their status to that of immigrant outside of the overall world ceiling. S. 2104 puts the immediate relatives of U.S. citizens as a first preference within the family reunification channel, capped at 470,000 visas. The Select Commission voted unanimously (including Senators Kennedy and Simpson, who otherwise spoke in favor of the principle of a cap) that immigration of spouses of U.S. citizens and their minor children should be exempt from numerical limitation (*See*, the revised tally of the votes of Select Commissioners of January 5, 1981).

Actually, the Commissioners voted to expand the exempt category by recommending (by a vote of fourteen to two) that the immigration of unmarried sons and daughters of U.S. citizens also be exempt from numerical limitation (Secretary of Labor Ray Marshall and Commissioner Jact Otero voted no), and that the grandparents of adult U.S. citizens should be exempt from numerical limitation, although without petitioning rights themselves until they had acquired citizenship (the vote was thirteen to three, with only Secretary Marshall, Secretary of Health and Human Services Patricia Roberts Harris, and Attorney General Benjamin Civiletti dissenting). The Select Commission was voted to continue the practice of allowing numerically unlimited entry of parents of adult U.S. citizens by a vote of sixteen to zero.

The Select Commission clearly intended to strengthen the petitioning privileges and rights of U.S citizens with respect to immediate family members, the major change being the abolition of the current first preference under numerically restricted immigration. S. 2104 clearly moves in an opposite direction with respect to that issue.

THE COMPARISION WITH RESPECT TO SECOND PREFERENCE

The Select Commission gave high priority to the reunification of the spouses and unmarried sons and daughters with their permanent resident alien relatives in the United States and recommended that a substantial number of visas should be set aside for this group and that it should be given top priority in the numerically limited family reunification category. Four Commissioners even believed that permanent resident aliens should have the same numerically exempt immigration status as those of U.S. citizens, but a large majority opposed that view. Indeed, three Commissioners voted to limit the immigration of sons and daughters only to those who are minors and unmarried.

S. 2104 follows the Select Commission recommendation that a substantial number of visas should be set aside for this group by doubling the number, which qualifies as a "substantial increase", but the preference is narrowed to include only spouses and unmarried children of permanent residents under the age of twenty-six, an approach which a majority of the Select Commissioners specifically rejected.

The most important difference in the approach of S. 2104 to current second preference and that of the Select Commission is that the present legislation retains per-country ceilings for the spouses and minor unmarried children of permanent resident aliens (under the age of twenty-six), whereas the Select Commission believed that it was extremely important to expedite family reunification for permanent resident aliens without regard to country ceilings.

Undoubtedly, some of the Commissioners probably had in mind the increased strain that would be placed on second preference by the legalization program recommended to deal with the then-existing stock of illegal aliens. Also, it was frequently mentioned in discussions that the failure to reunify immediate relatives, particularly in Mexico and other places close to the United States, created an enormous incentive for illegal migration. Moreover, it was generally thought that it was bad policy to make individuals wait to be reunited with their spouses or minor children simply because of their nationality while others of a difference nationality could be reunited more quickly. This was not just a matter of equity for the individuals involved, but something that would be in the best interests of the communities in which they lived and of the United States as a whole.

OTHER COMPARISONS ON FAMILY REUNIFICATION

The Selection Commission also recommended that the adult sons and daughters of permanent resident aliens be accorded a separate preference for family reunification visas with per-country ceilings applying to that group. Also, the Select Commission recommended that a limited preference be given to the elderly parents of permanent resident aliens. Such elderly parents — if they had no children living outside the United States — would be eligible for a small percentage of the family reunification visas available annually.

There is no question that S. 2104 continues to give great weight to family reunification by reserving 470,000 visas within that track. The Select Commission recommendations calling for 250,000 numerically restricted family reunification immigrants plus the numerically exempt immediate relatives of U.S. citizens would not provide a larger number of visas for family reunification immigrants at first, but by maintaining the numerically exempt category, that number would grow, particularly under the impact of legalization. While that point is not at all troubling to me, it may be precisely the point that led so many Senators to accept the principle of a cap on all relatives.

MORE COMPARISON: THE ISSUE OF THE BACKLOGS

The Select Commission was also more open to family reunification by recommending the clearance of backlogs at the rate of 100,000 a year for five years in conjuncton of the introduction of legalization and the new lawful admissions system, something that would ease pressure on the second and fifth preferences particulary. In this connection, if one assumes that second preference should be given much greater weight and fifth preference lesser weight or none at all, S. 2104 can be seen as more constructive than the Select Commission's recommendations, since its modification of fifth preference may make the total numbers of visas available in second preference larger than would have been the case under the system proposed by the Select Commission, which was concerned not just with the expansion of second preference but with the elimination of country ceilings concerning second preference and (by a close vote) with retaining fifth preference in its present form.

INDEPENDENT IMMIGRANTS AND THEIR SELECTION

The approach of S. 2104 and of the Select Commission is similar in several respects. S. 2104 allocates 120,000 visas for independent immigrants, compared to 100,000 stipulated by the staff of the Select Commission under the guidelines set forth by the Commissioners. Both the Commission and S. 2104 call for the entry of a small, numerically limited category of immigrants with exceptional qualifications. Both recommend a small number of investors (although Father Theodore S. Hesburgh, Chairman of the Commission, expressed strong oppsition). Neither recommends a special provision for the immigration of retirees.

S. 2104 provides that 55,000 independent immigrants be admitted according to a point system, a method of selection that won only two votes on the Select Commission (Representative Robert McClory (R-Illinois) and Senator Simpson). Most Commissioners preferred either a revision of the present labor certification procedure and a requirement that prospective immigrants to the U.S. have a job offer or a revision of the labor certification procedure to make prospective independent immigrants admissible unless the Secretary of Labor had certified that there already were sufficient numbers of American workers or resident aliens available to do the kind of work sought by the would-be immigrant. This last method would not require a U.S. job offer.

COMPARISON ON THE NATIONAL ORIGINS ISSUE

Some of the sponsors of S. 2104 made clear that one of their intentions is to encourage immigration from Europe, particularly for highly skilled, educated and English-speaking men and women. At the Select Commission, no thought was voiced concerning the national origins of independent immigrants. All of the discussion was about the most desirable characteristics of such immigrants, regardless of nationality. Fortunately, S. 2104 does not give points to anyone for being a national of a nation alleged to have been harmed by the 1965 amendments to the Immigration and Nationality Act, since the concept of adversely affected nations was a surrogate for national origins preference. The point system embodied in S. 2104 may open up some immigration from certain European countries disproportionate to immigration from other countries, but actually the point system may not yield a higher proportion of European immigrants than Filipinos, West Indies or even Chinese than the methods of selection suggested by the Select Commission. The overall effect of all of these methods will be the same: to open immigration to persons regardless of their national origins who do not have the basis for family reunification to become immigrants to the United States. The Select Commission's methods, particularly one of them, would have relied much more on self-selection than on points given according to some ascribed criteria.

Neither approach will radically alter the nationality composition of immigrants or change a system which heavily favors those who are connected, either by family or education or job contacts, and who therefore are much more highly skilled and cosmopolitan and more adaptable to American life than the ancestor-immigrants of the vast majority of us sitting in this room.

Some of the Select Commissioners, such as Secretary of Health and Human Services Patricia Roberts Harris, talked about returning to the old days when an ordinary peasant or worker could come to the United States. But existing policy favors the already favored. Yet, it still calls for a large measure of self selection, and the human initiative, energy and enterprise that goes with that.

IMPROVING S. 2104

It will not come as a surprise that I believe that S. 2104 can be improved to some extent by looking more carefully at where it differs from the recommendation of the Select Commission and by giving careful consideration to those recommendations in amending it. Given the continuation of low fertility rates in the United States, a strong and stable civic culture which unites Americans of diverse backgrounds, and the responsibilities of the United States as a world power, it probably would be to the interest of this nation to accept even a larger number of immigrants than that contemplated by the recommendations of the Select Commission or by the provisions of S. 2104. This is not the time to include immediate relatives within an overall cap on immigration. It probably would be wise to expand numerically restricted immigration to at least the level of 350,000 proposed by the Select Commission. From my own reading of American society, and its needs, potentialities, and resposibilities as we move toward the twenty-first century, it seems to me that we could benefit greatly by an additional expansion of 50,000 assigned to the independent category. The very best and the brightest want to come to the United States. My own strong view is that the strengthening of this nation through immigration will benefit not just Americans but others as well, not just because of remittances sent home by immigrants but because of the transfer of knowledge and expansion of international contacts in business and education that take place beween ethnic-Americans and the citizens of their ancestral homelands over a period of generations following initial immigration. It has never been more true than now that the United States can do well for itself and the world by doing good through a positive approach to immigration.

10

Humanitarian Admissions:
A Gap in U.S. Immigration Policy

SUSAN FORBES MARTIN
Senior Associate, Refugee Policy Group, Washington, D.C.

DURING the past two decades, the United States has addressed many issues related to immigration: the bases for legal immigration; policies for the admission and assistance of refugees from overseas; options to control the flow of undocumented aliens to the United States; and most recently, the standard to be used in determining if an individual should be granted asylum. My colleagues have or will discuss additional changes that are needed in these areas. I am limiting my remarks to a major issue that still goes unresolved: the admission of people on humanitarian grounds. The issue takes two forms: 1) the admission of people from overseas who do not meet the refugee definition but who are of special concern to this country; and 2) the handling of those seeking a safe haven from potentially dangerous situations who arrive directly to the United States.

ADMISSIONS FROM OVERSEAS

For much of the post World War II period, the United States has responded to the need for admission from overseas of people fleeing life-threatening situations through resettlement programs operated under special legislation or the Attorney General's parole authority. This country has resettled millions of refugees and others who left their countries of origin and sought asylum in neighboring countries before receiving permission to come to the United States. It was through resettlement channels that the large scale admissions of displaced persons after World War II, Hungarians in 1956, Cubans in the 1960s and 1970s and Southeast Asians in 1975 took place. After years of *ad hoc* arrangements for resettlement, the Refugee Act of 1980 established a formal system for the admission of refugees from overseas through an annual consultation process involving the President and Congress.

Prior to 1980, whether individuals met the strict definition of a refugee was less important in determining their admissibility than the overall circumstances in which they found themselves. In other words, members of certain groups could be admitted as parolees without requiring that they as individuals demonstrate their refugee credentials. This procedure enabled the United States to move quickly and effectively to meet humanitarian objectives.

However, it also gave the Attorney General, acting without consultation, broad discretionary powers and to replace the *ad hoc* nature of refugee decision-making with an orderly and consultative process. Accordingly, they drafted a new law prohibiting the Attorney General from paroling refugee groups or individual refugees into the country unless he or she "determines that compelling reasons in the public interest with respect to that particular alien require that the alien be paroled into the United States rather than be admitted as a refugee..." (Section 203 (B)).

At present, there are no admissions programs to serve the humanitarian concerns of this country, beyond individual refugee admissions. Without the option of large-scale parole programs, there are only two ways that people can gain legal, permanent entry to the United States: as immigrants or as refugees (and asylees). However, immigration policies, for practical purpo ses, have since 1965 been focused on people with close family ties to the United States and people with essential labor skills. While the need to open immigration channels to other individuals has been debated (most recently regarding the proposed changes in the legal immigration system sponsored by Senators Kennedy and Simpson), the discussions have focused primarily on regional balances and/or labor force criteria not humanitarian grounds.

The U.S. refugee program remains the only program through which persons of humanitarian concern can be admitted to this country. Yet, it is designed for persons who individually meet refugee criteria not for large groups of people in emergency situations, even if these situations are politically rooted. Adhering strictly to the procedures outlined in the Act, it would be difficult to mount a rescue operation today similar to the 1979 Indochinese program in which the United States admitted some 14,000 Southeast Asians per month. Should the United States government wish to admit large numbers of people dislocated because of civil disorder, military attacks, or natural disaster, it may have to do so once more by using the Attorney General's parole authority or by misusing the refugee program and admitting people who might not meet the definition.

Current mechanisms also present difficulties in addressing the situations of individuals who do not themselves meet the refugee definition, but are in refugee-like situations. Amerasians are one such example. Some may be unable to demonstrate refugee bonafides but all are still of humanitarian interest to this nation. Because of the lack of a category for admitting these people, it has taken special legislation to meet the need for resettlement of Amerasians who do not fit the refugee definition.

Recently, this gap in admissions provisions became apparent with regard to Armenians released from the Soviet Union. On the one hand, the loosening of restrictions on emigration represents a major foreign policy victory for the United States. On the other, when faced with thousands of Armenians with exit visas, the United States has had to resort to the refugee admissions program — even though by all reports the Armenians are not claiming fear of persecution — because there is no other mechanism for the entry.

DIRECT ARRIVALS

U.S. policies for handling direct arrivals of migrants who have fled potentially life-threatening situations are also inadequate. Direct arrival of political migrants has increasingly been a factor in U.S. immigration policy during the past two decades, beginning with the Cuban exiles of the 1960s. In fact, within a few months of passage of the Refugee Act of 1980, 125,000 Cubans arrived on our shores and sought refuge. Since then, thousands of others from throughout the world have sought political asylum,; many others have remained illegally in this country, requesting relief from deportation only if thev are apprehended.

The current system is neither able to offer sufficient access to the protections that, on humanitarian grounds, the United States could afford, nor does it allow for adequate control of U.S. borders. Its inadequacy results in large part from a failure to come to terms with the fact that the United States is, and is likely to remain a country of first asylum for individuals who migrate for both economic and political reasons.

Among the groups most at risk under the current policy are those who have left life-threatening circumstances but who do not seek or qualify for permanent asylum. Their characteristics, as elaborated by Alexander Aleinikoff of the University of Michigan Law School before the House Immigration Subcommittee are:

1) persons from a country experiencing civil war, a general breakdown of public order, or occupation by a foreign power;

2) Persons likely to suffer substantial infringement of human rights if returned home, where such treatment cannot be considered persecution based on religious belief, race, nationality or membership on a social group; and

3) Persons in this country who do not choose to apply for asylum...because they would like to return to their home countries once conditions change or are fearful that their applications will not be fairly adjudicated here."

Recent court cases have held that there is no obligation to consider asylum for those fleeing situations of civil conflict, widespread violence or anarchy if persecution is not a factor. In cases involving Salvadoran refugees, for example, the Board of Immigration Appeals (BIA) held that the applicants were more akin to "refugees" within the meaning of the Refugee Act that governs asylum determinations. According to the BIA, "there must be a showing that the claimed persecution is *on account* of the group's identifying characteristics." Such a determination is difficult for many political migrants, particularly those from countries with civil strife. As one recent report on Central America noted:

Central American refugees (sic) are not individually persecuted for reasons of religion, race or political opinion, in many cases. Generally speaking, the problem is not one of convictions *per se*, but rather, something much more basic and thus much more tragic: having to save one's life without even knowing why it is endangered.[1]

Faced with the inadequacy of the asylum system for dealing with humanitarian concerns when migrants are not refugees, the United States have granted safe haven to members of some nationalities, albeit on a discretionary basis. Others having benefitted from "benign neglect," are allowed to remain illegally in this country because the government has neither the capacity nor the will to find and deport them. These recurring practices have not amounted to a coherent, consistent policy, however. Instead, the United States has used *ad hoc* mechanisms, relying on political, ideological and foreign policy factors that may or may not take into account the actual circumstances from which those in need of safe haven have fled.

There has been little opportunity to debate the criteria for granting safe haven or the form that safe haven should take. Today, such debate is especially important because of the potential controls on immigration that may stem from passage or the Immigration Reform and Control Act (IRCA). Under IRCA it is illegal to hire undocumented aliens. Also, there is increased emphasis on border enforcement. The effects of the law are being felt even before full implementation. For example, newspapers report that undocumented aliens have been fired from their jobs; larger numbers of Salvadorans, fearful of their ability to remain legally or illegally in the United States, have been seeking refuge in Canada.

THE NEED FOR LEGISLATIVE RESPONSES

There is a need for a mechanism recognized in statute, separate from refugee admissions, asylum and withholding of deportation, through which individuals and groups who do not meet the refugee definition can receive permission to enter or remain in the United States because of humanitarian considerations. The existing administrative remedies are clearly insufficient. And, the only clear statutory basis for admitting individuals on humanitarian grounds requires that the alien meets the refugee definition. Yet, the refugee definition, as discussed, does not cover the range of humanitarian circumstances from which political exiles may need temporary or permanent protection. Nor does it cover the range of individuals to whom the United States may wish to provide temporary or permanent status.

The reasons for leaving one's home country or being afraid to return are far more complex than those covered in the refugee definition. Many migrants who do not have a well-founded fear of persecution nevertheless have a well-founded fear of injury, deprivation of human rights and even death. They have left situations of civil war, civil strife and repression where there is a good likelihood that they could be the victim of random or organized violence. The United States has traditionally shown compassion for such individuals and it is likely that this nation will be called upon to offer refuge in future humanitarian emergencies. Having a statutory basis through which humanitarian admissions or safe haven can be granted will provide an orderly process through which the United States can respond, to what we know are recurrent phenomena.

Without a statutory basis for admitting those of special humanitarian concern, decisions are likely to continue to be made on purely discretionary bases. Or, as several government officials have noted, in the absence of a firm legislative and regulatory base, mid-level staff will continue to make difficult decisions without having adequate standards or guidelines. Or decisions will be politicized, with short-term foreign policy and immigration ramifications receiving greater attention than humanitarian factors. And finally, with the courts unable to review decisions to ensure that they meet agreed-upon standards.

In any legislation developed, there will be a need to balance executive branch discretion and legislative/judicial oversight in making decisions about humanitarian admissions. Here, there would be many advantages to preserving a large measure of executive discretion properly monitored by the legislative branch, most importantly to maintain the flexibility to respond quickly to emergent situations.

Within the refugee resettlement programs, there is a consultative process that ensures Presidential and Congressional discussion of admission issues prior to the start of each fiscal year. While our previous research has shown some weaknesses in current practice regarding these consultations (they are not timely; provide inadequate input from groups outside of government; and do not make sufficiently clear the criteria used in assessing the need for resettlement), they have served the purpose of increasing communication between the two branches of government. With some changes in law and practice to address these weaknesses, the consultative process could provide an appropriate mechanism for making decisions about humanitarian admissions as well as safe haven.

Also needed are legislated criteria against which to measure the decisions made by the executive branch. The criteria to be used in determining the need for humanitarian admissions or temporary safe haven must take into account a variety of factors: humanitarian concerns, foreign policy, and immigration. It is the weight given to the various factors that is key. Through the process of developing legislation, these criteria should be debated, bringing a variety of perspectives to bear.

Finally, decisions on humanitarian admissions and safe haven should be addressed in the context of efforts to internationalize refugee and related problems. By definition, refugee and refugee-like situations denote movement across national boundaries and therefore involve more than one country. Decisions regarding humanitarian admissions should take greater account of the impact of these decisions on other countries' policies and standards for the protection of refugees and persons in refugee-like situations. For example, the unwillingness of the United States to provide safe haven can have negative impacts on practices and standards of other countries. Countries of first asylum, such as Thailand, Pakistan and Mexico which provide safe haven to thousands of individuals coming from neighboring countries, may see U.S. rejection of asylum seekers from nearby countries such as El Salvador and Haiti as a justification for more restrictive policies.

To conclude, as this nation moves forward in addressing the range of immigration issues discussed today, attention should be paid to this major gap in existing legislation. We have had a strong tradition as a haven for those who would otherwise be endangered. U.S. legislation should reflect this permanent commitment to humanitarian admissions.

FOOTNOTES

[1] Edelberto Torres-Rivas, Report on the Condition of Central American Refugees and Migrants, July 1985, p. 14.

11

H.R.5115 and S.2104: Legislation to Reform Legal Immigration [1]

WARREN R. LEIDEN
Executive Director, American Immigration Lawyers Association

IN the almost ten years since the original deliberations of the Select Commission on Immigration and Refugee Policy began, we believe that a number of fundamental principles have emerged that are essential to the reform of legal immigration to the United States.

Immigration Sponsored by a U.S. Family Member or Employer Should Continue to be the Major Source of Newcomers to the United States

United States immigration law and policy has, for some time, strongly favored lawful immigration sponsored by a U.S. family member or employer. We think it is important to reaffirm the principle that the fundamental and major source of future immigration should be individually sponsored, whether for family unification or for employment purposes.

The benefits of family- and employer-sponsored immigration are several:

First, sponsored immigration directly and immediately benefits the national interest by promoting unification of American families and by encouraging economic development where labor certification has shown a shortage of U.S. workers;

Second, unlike the indirect benefits of non-sponsored, independent immigration, employer-sponsored immigration is based on a real job with a known employer after a direct test of the availability of U.S. workers, at wages and working conditions that will not adversely affect other U.S. workers;

Third, family and employer sponsors help newcomer immigrants learn the ropes of social and economic life in the United States, thereby promoting early and efficient acculturation; and

Finally, an immigrant's sponsor is a direct source of financial support and domestic assistance to the immigrant upon arrival, either through family resources or actual employment, thereby minimizing reliance on public funds.

Family unification has, for decades, been the fundamental precept of immigration to the United States. AILA renews its support for a U.S. immigration policy that recognizes the crucial value of families as a fundamental unit of our society.

Employer-sponsored immigration under the present third and sixth preferences has provided important human resources to U.S. employers where the Department of Labor has certified there are no qualified U.S. workers available. In addition to the tightly-monitored recruitment process, the law requires employer-sponsors to pay wages and maintain working conditions that will not adversely affect other U.S. workers.

Although it is sometimes called "independent", employer-sponsored immigration admits immigrant workers for whom there is an immediate need in the United States, sponsored and paid for by the employer who actually needs the worker. Thus, while we don't dispute the value of statistical and demographic studies that predict general labor needs in the future, they should not be substituted as the major determinant of employment-related immigration needs.

Immediate Relatives of U.S. Citizens Should Not Be Set Off Against Other Family-Sponsored Immigrants, Nor Placed Under An Absolute Ceiling or Cap

Present law relating to sponsored immigration provides for two basic categories: numerically-limited categories, including the six preferences for family-sponsored and employer-sponsored immigration, and the non-numerically restricted category for "immediate relatives" of U.S. citizens, which includes minor children, spouses, and parents of adult U.S. citizens.

Whether by a quota, cap, or set-off against other family categories, numerical restrictions on immediate relatives of U.S. citizens should be rejected. Placing such restrictions on immediate relatives - the most close and intimate family relationship recognized by our immigration laws - would strike a major blow against family unification as the major source of immigration to the United States.

Family unification has long been and should continue to be the fundamental basis and purpose of immigration to the United States. An immigration policy that fosters family unification not only pays respect to tradition, but it also makes a concrete statement about the values our nation takes into the future. There is no more fundamental building block of society, nor more important nor intimate relationship than that between immediate family members.

It could also be said that family unification is the strongest type of immigration, in that the newcomer to America is welcomed by those with the greatest interest in his or her success and acclimation. It is well known among immigration practitioners that immigrant families will go to great lengths to provide support and assistance to their close relatives, both upon arrival and long into the future.

The introduction of a cap or set-off of immediate relatives against other family members eligible for immigration would tend to fragment and divide individual families and would damage how we, as a nation, value family relations. We hope this Committee will reject the proposal that family unification must now be restricted by placing limits on immediate relatives.

Modest Increases in Annual Immigrant Admissions Are in the National Interest

Almost eight years ago, following the most recent study of its kind, the Select Commission on Immigration and Refugee Policy recommended that annual, numerically-restricted immigration be increased to 350,000 admissions per year, plus at least 100,000 more admissions per year to reduce backlogs in the various preference categories.

Although we hold the view that a new, comprehensive study of immigration policy is warranted, we believe the recommendation to modestly increase immigration will promote the national interest. While AILA does not presume to claim expertise in population or demographic analysis, it is plain from a variety of sources, such as *Workforce 2000*, that modest increases in immigration are not only warranted, but that they will become necessary to meet the social and economic needs of the U.S. in an era of shrinking birth rates and an aging population.

We therefore support legislation that will provide reasonable increases in annual legal immigration.

The Existing Family-Sponsored and Employer-Sponsored Preference Categories Should Not Be Changed Until the Legalization Program and Employer Sanctions Have Been Evaluated.

Consistent with the recommendations of the Select Commission, we firmly believe that no changes should be made to the existing family-sponsored or employer-sponsored preference categories until there has been an opportunity to evaluate fully the consequences of the legalization program and employer sanctions enacted in the Immigration Reform and Control Act of 1986.

As attorneys practicing immigration law, AILA members are familiar with hundreds of thousands of immigrant cases, both family-sponsored and employer-sponsored. In our judgment, both the legalization and employer sanction programs are having a profound effect on the needs of U.S. immigrant sponsors, as well as on those who seek to immigrate to the U.S.

Ultimately, all preference categories for immigration are arbitrary, based on the political choices of a nation. The present preference categories have stood the test of time, and have promoted the national interest by both reflecting the interests of U.S. sponsors and the desires of intending immigrants.

We believe there is no basis to eliminate or reduce any of the existing family categories, all of which relate to relationships between spouses, parents and children, and among children.

The employer-sponsored categories — aliens of exceptional ability in the arts and sciences, members of the professions, and skilled and experienced unskilled workers — are relied on by many U.S. enterprises for crucial employees not available in the U.S. workforce.

We believe that the employer sanctions program is having a significant impact on employment relations and the availability of workers at the highest and lowest levels. Until this program has been fully implemented and its results evaluated, it would be a mistake to make changes that might only have to be undone in several years.

Until the new immigration reform programs are fully evaluated, there is no basis to eliminate or cut back the existing immigrant preference categories.

Backlogs of Qualified Applicants Do Not Constitute a Reason to Eliminate An Eligibility Category

Some of the current preference categories are substantially backlogged, particularly for the six "oversubscribed" countries (China, India, Korea, Mexico, the Dominican Republic, and the Philippines). It has been suggested that the existence of such backlogs is a reason to eliminate some categories of eligibility. Frankly, we think this is illogical.

Our members are quite familiar with both the sponsors and beneficiaries of petitions that have been backlogged. While no one is happy about the present situation, those who are patiently and lawfully waiting in line do not think they are being helped by those who propose taking away their immigrant eligibility. The day upon which many immigrants can come to the United States is an important ray of hope that is not diminished by the time they must wait. If Congress is to act in the interest of these persons and their U.S. sponsors by reducing backlogs, it must reform current law by increasing admissions, not by telling these beneficiaries that they are no longer eligible.

We are also aware that some qualified applicants may have already become eligible for lawful status in the United States through the legalization program or other immigrant categories. This is another reason why changes should not be made to the preference categories until the legalization program is fully evaluated.

The national origin quota system was eliminated in 1965. It is only since that time that immigrants from certain countries began to be permitted in equal numbers. Given the fact that there has been only one generation of immigration from those countries, it is difficult to escape the conclusion that elimination of certain preference categories at this time is aimed directly at preventing more of their kind from coming to the United States.

If there must be changes to the preference categories, let them be made on a deliberate and reasoned basis, not simply because of the existence of a waiting line or backlog of qualified applicants.

With Appropriate Selection Criteria, Non-Sponsored, Independent Immigration Could Promote Diversity and Fairness.

Although AILA favors sponsored immigration as the major source of immigrants, we believe an effective case can be made for including within our legal immigration scheme some non-sponsored, independent immigration. Immigration not tied to a sponsor could provide some diversity by making eligible persons whose families have not already come to the United States. An independent, selected-immigrant program could also permit some additional immigration from nations whose greatest numbers of immigrants came to the United States generations ago. Moreover, the right kind of independent selection program could give a wider variety of individuals some chance at immigrating and becoming a contributing member of American life.

In our view, however, the selection system for non-sponsored immigrants should not place undue weight on any single characteristic. For instance, while admitting highly educated individuals is certainly one goal, we are also respectful of the historic immigrant characteristics of initiative, drive, and willingness to work hard. If current studies pointing to a future shortage of lower-skilled workers are even partially correct, it would be a mistake to skew independent immgration solely toward highly-educated, highly-skilled persons.

It is our experience that employer-sponsored immigration is the best and most direct way to secure needed, highly-skilled workers. With so many occupations today requiring university or advanced education, independent immigration based simply on levels of education does not provide the targeted selection that is the foundation of employer-sponsored immigration.

We are also mindful of some of the weaknesses of non-sponsored immigration. Independent immigrants have no sponsor to help them acclimate or fit into American society. True, many may already be familiar with our ways and want to immigrate on that basis, but this should not be a basis for major reform in immigration policy. Moreover, with no family or employer sponsor, the question of employment and financial support for non-sponsored immigrants is left open. We are not aware of any proposals for appropriations for resettlement of non-sponsored, independent immigrants, but we are skeptical that much support could be found.

Also, although they would be permitted to enter the United States because of certain employment-related characteristics, no one knows what jobs independent immigrants would actually take, how quickly they would find them, and for how long they would keep them.

AILA strongly opposes any independent immigrant category that seeks to deliberately favor one nationality over another so as to reinstitute a form of national origin discrimination in our immigration law and policy. A shameful era in our nation's history ended in 1965 with the abolition of restrictions on immigration from certain nationalities and geographical regions. Measures that would reintroduce such preferences should be rejected.

Numerical Limits and Eligibility Categories for Legal Immigration Should Only be Changed Through the Normal Legislative Process

As the Committee is well aware, some of our immigration laws and policy have remained unchanged for too long, in part because of the controversial nature of the subject and in part because of other priorities. In addition, we believe there have not always been the kind of facts and analyses of the causes and consequences of annual immigration to the United States that should be the basis of proposals for change. We therefore strongly support proposals to institute regular periodic study of immigration to the United States and its effects on our national life.

AILA cannot, however, support proposals that would permit an automatic or mechanistic change in annual immigrant admissions or the preference categories whenever Congress is not able to act on such recommendations. In our opinion, the difficulty that Congress may occasionally have in enacting immigration legislation reflects the serious thought and consideration this subject deserves. While there is some attraction to having an automatic mechanism that would provide needed change when Congress is unable to act in a short period of time, we are more convinced than ever that taking no action is preferable to enacting recommendations not subject to the checks and balances of the legislative process.

We are mindful of emergency situations in which, for short periods of time, there exists a popular revulsion or xenophobic response toward immigrants based on a momentary event or crisis. It would be a tragedy if an automatic mechanism to change immigration admissions were to come into play precisely at the time of a short-lived immigration emergency.

As noted above, AILA generally supports modest increases in annual immigrant admissions. We are willing to forego the possibility of further increases through an automatic mechanism, to avoid the risk of untimely reductions in immigration under the same system. Having wrestled with this subject for some time, we are of the firm conclusion that only the regular legislative process will ensure the national interest in setting annual immigrant admissions levels.

COMMENTS ON THE RODINO-MAZZOLI BILL — H.R. 5115, LEGAL IMMIGRATION AMENDMENTS OF 1988

The following section will focus on our association's analysis of H.R. 5115, the Legal Immigration Amendments of 1988, co-sponsored by Chairmen

Rodino and Mazzoli. Our analysis tracks the bill section-by-section and provides some description as well as our judgment on each proposal.

First, however, we must acknowledge what the Rodino-Mazzoli bill does not contain. To the great credit of the sponsors, H.R. 5115 neither imposes a ceiling on the annual admissions of immediate relatives of U.S. citizens nor sets off such immigrants against other family-sponsored immigration. Moreover, the Rodino bill does not eliminate any portions of the current preference categories, either family-sponsored or employer-sponsored. Furthermore, H.R. 5115 puts into place an important Commission to study U.S. immigration that will provide the facts and analyses necessary before making more comprehensive reform.

For these reasons, as well as for the positive changes that are detailed below, AILA is pleased to lend its endorsement of Rodino-Mazzoli legal immigration reform bill, H.R. 5115.

H.R. 5115-Section 2, Worldwide Level of Independent Immigrants

AILA supports the bill's separation of family-sponsored preference categories from employer-sponsored categories, with separate annual ceilings.

Under present law, the third and sixth employer-sponsored immigrant preferences are allocated an annual total of 54,000 visas. H.R. 5115 would increase these amounts and add several new eligibility categories, with an aggregate annual total of 150,000 visas per year. The bill would also establish a national commission on independent immigration with five members appointed by the President, charged with examining the effect of both employer-sponsored and non-sponsored selected independent immigrants.

Every other year beginning January, 1992, the commission would recommend an annual independent immigrant total, but not less than 75,000, nor more than 225,000 per year. Congress would be provided with an expedited procedure under which to take action on this recommendation; if it does not act, the recommendation could take effect automatically.

AILA members are particularly sensitive to the ebb and flow of demand for employer-sponsored immigrants. H.R. 5115's increases in annual admissions for employer-sponsored immigrants would better satisfy the needs for key personnel of businesses and industry and would help to continue America's economic and technological leadership. The bill's new non-family categories and the allocation of annual admissions among them is addressed below.

AILA also strongly supports proposals for studies and reports of annual immigration, its effect on the United States, and the variety of needs and factors that are reasonably related to legal immigration. We support the provision in H.R. 5115 for a study of independent immigration, and we encourage its application to all legal immigration, to the degree not provided for by the Immigration Reform and Control Act of 1986. Nonetheless, we strongly prefer that the recommendations and reports of the national commission not include an automatic mechanism to change the overall independent immigrant admissions, absent action by Congress.

We also urge that additional factors be considered in the commission's report, such as the number and types of petitions for employer-sponsored immigration, in addition to the point system program.

H.R. 5115-Section 3, Revision of the Independent Immigration Preference System

Building on the current third and sixth immigrant preference categories, the Rodino-Mazzoli bill sets out three new independent immigrant classifications, including both employer-sponsored and non-sponsored immigrants. Each of the three new independent categories would receive one-third of the total admissions — 50,000 visas per year.

First Independent Category (Third Preference)

The first independent category includes members of the professions and immigrants of exceptional ability in the sciences, arts, or education. Essentially, this category is identical to the present third preference category and includes the most highly educated and skilled aliens admitted to the United States. Immigrants qualifying under this category must have an employer sponsor whose job offer they are accepting, although the Attorney General is provided the authority to waive the job offer requirement when deemed to be in the national interest, which occurs in the case of artists and others who are largely self-employed. As under current law, the employer sponsor would be required to seek the Secretary of Labor's certification that there are no qualified U.S. workers available and that the wages and working conditions offered would not adversely affect other U.S. workers.

Second Independent Category (Sixth Preference, Investors, Retirees)

The second independent immigrant category includes three parts. The first sub-category includes the present sixth preference, for aliens capable of specific skilled or unskilled labor where the Secretary of Labor has certified there are not qualified, willing, and able U.S. workers for the positions. The second sub-category includes job-creating investors who invest at least $500,000 and whose investment creates at least ten jobs for U.S. citizens or permanent residents other than the investor's immediate family. The third sub-category includes retirees who are not seeking employment.

AILA strongly supports the inclusion of these three sub-categories of immigrant eligibility. As stated above, we do not think there should be any changes to the existing preference categories until the effects of legalization and employer sanctions can be fully evaluated; thus we endorse preserving the existing sixth preference category for specified skilled and unskilled labor under the first sub-category.

As the Committee knows, the employer sponsors of skilled and unskilled workers are obliged to comply with the stringent requirements of the Department of Labor. Moreover, although some of the occupations covered are described as "unskilled", in fact, aliens immigrating on this basis are required to have paid experience overseas in the occupation to qualify to immigrate. As was recently pointed out, preserving the existing sixth preference category for skilled and unskilled immigrants permits working-class aliens to enter the United Sates, thereby continuing an important historic tradition.

Skilled and unskilled immigrant workers are needed for a variety of positions in short supply in the U.S. economy. These include technicians, specialized crafts workers, and skilled designers in both productive industry and in research and development. In the service sector, sixth preference beneficiaries include religious workers, specialty chefs and cooks, home-care attendants for the elderly and disabled, as well as domestic workers employed by families.

AILA also strongly supports the sub-category for job-creating investors. We particularly commend the sponsors for setting the threshold investment amount at $500,000. In our experience, and based on discussions with state economic development agencies, this amount is more in line with the capital needs of a new enterprise expected to employ at least ten U.S. workers and continue to grow and create further employment.

Finally, AILA endorses the re-establishment of an immigrant preference category for self-supporting retirees who do not intend to seek gainful employment in the United States. Unfortunately, the practical demise of the former immigrant category for retirees has obliged individuals who wish to retire in the United States to enter and remain only as long as they qualify for a visitor's visa. This provision would remedy that unfortunate situation.

Although we support each of these sub-categories, we are concerned that there is no priority or designated allocation among them. That is, employer-sponsored immigrants would be, in a sense, competing with non-sponsored investors and retirees for the same annual allotment of visas. In a "worst case" situation, employer-sponsored skilled and unskilled immigrants could be cut back below the current levels of admission. We recommend that the sponsors separate the employer-sponsored sub-category from the non-sponsored sub-categories under separate annual admissions numbers. Provision should be made that the equivalent of the present sixth preference directly receives no fewer than the current 27,000 visas per year and that visas not used by the new first independent category "spill down" and be made available for these employer-sponsored immigrants.

Third Independent Category (Point System Immigrants)

The last independent category would permit the immigration of aliens who score at least 30 points under a system that awards points for youth, education, occupational shortage, additional training, and pre-arranged employment.

As indicated above, AILA supports this experiment with non-sponsored independent immigration based on broad, general characteristics, although we continue to believe that employer-sponsored immigration remains the most useful and efficient means of locating needed personnel for the U.S. economy. Because the proposed system would give preference to those aliens who scored the greatest number of points, we suggest that the education qualification provide some points for aliens who have completed the equivalent of a high school or elementary school education, to diversify those eligible.

Under our reading of the point system, no alien gets the 30 points needed to qualify for independent immigration unless he or she is qualified in an occupation for which the Secretary of Labor determines there will be a shortage of able, willing, and qualified individuals in the U.S. in that occupation for the following two year period. This proposal breaks entirely new ground for U.S. immgration policy, and we think there needs to be special attention and concern paid to the process and results of these general occupational shortage determinations. Despite diligence and all the best intentions, it is not clear that the Labor Department could adequately identify a wide variety of possible occupations to make a sufficient number of occupational shortage determinations within the time periods required.

We believe it is appropriate and necessary that there be a special national commission on independent immigration studying and making recommendations as discussed above. However, as presently written, the national commission is charged with setting annual admissions numbers that will apply automatically under the one-third/one-third/one-third formula. Thus, any changes to independent admissions will affect not ony the non-sponsored independent point system immigrants but will also directly increase or reduce visas available for the other two categories of "independent" immigrants: employer-sponsored immigration for exceptional ability aliens, members of the professions, skilled and unskilled workers, and job-creating investors and retirees.

In other words, the commission under this bill could not recommend reducing the number of independent immigrants under the point system without proportionally reducing the number of admissions per year under the other two categories. Because we are particularly sensitive to the contrast between employer-sponsored immigrants and non-sponsored, independent immigrants, we believe it would be a mistake to keep them in the "same boat".

AILA urges the sponsors to consider an amendment that would, 1) preserve the employer-sponsored immigrants in a single category with its own annual admissions number and, 2) establish a separate category for the non-sponsored, independent immigrants including job-creating investors, retirees, and point system selected immigrants. The national commission would also study and make recommendations on this non-sponsored, independent category.

In-Country Distribution for Countries at Per Country Ceiling

H.R. 5115 would reallocate worldwide annual admissions between the family-sponsored immigrant categories on the one hand and the employer-sponsored and non-sponsored immigrant categories on the other. It is therefore appropriate to similarly reallocate the so-called "per country" immigration levels between the two categories, by amending Section 202 of the INA.

The bill provides that if immigration from one country reaches the "per country" limit of 20,000, those visas must be allocated between family-sponsored and "independent" immigrants at a ratio of 1.44 to one, which is the ratio of overall family preferences (216,000) to "independents" (150,000).

Under this formula, the six "oversubscribed" countries (China, the Dominican Republic, India, Korea, Mexico, and the Philippines), which annually reach or almost reach the 20,000 limit, would be limited to fewer than 12,000 family admissions but would be permitted more than 8,000 independent admissions. Unfortunately, this would represent a cut-back of up to 6,000 family admissions per year for those countries based on FY 1986 statistics.

Assuming the goal is to preserve family immigration at "per country" levels no less than present, this unintended consequence could be remedied in several ways. Probably the most appealing alternative would be to provide a modest increase in the "per country" ceiling, say to 23,000, and to employ a family-to-independent ratio of four to one (based on the present ration between family-sponsored and employer-sponsored preference immigrants). Other than perhaps dedicating 15,000 of the new 96,000 visas to the six oversubscribed countries (if present demand continues), these changes would have little effect on admissions from any other countries.

Revision of Labor Certification

In two fundamental ways, H.R. 5115 would amend INS Section 212(a) (14) relating to permanent labor certification. First, the recruitment test of the labor market for qualified U.S. workers would become national in scope unless, in its discretion, the Labor Department permitted recruitment more tailored to the nature of the actual job and its location. This latter, more flexible standard is used under present law. Currently, the Labor Department can require national recruitment for jobs or job locations where that is the usual practice for recruiting U.S. workers (e.g., professionals, scientists, mobile labor), while requiring only regional recruitment for positions that are normally filled from the region.

The other major change to labor certification would be permitting the use of labor market information (statistics) without recruitment for a specific job.

If statistics would lead to denial of the certification, the employer could submit evidence that an individual labor certification would result differently.

The permanent labor certification process - which is responsible for testing the availability of U.S. workers for a particular job - is complicated and often seems quite inefficient. In New York and several areas of the country, permanent labor certification now takes about two years to complete.

However, we are not convinced that changing the scope of recruitment from the present flexible standard to a national standard (albeit with discretion) is an improvement in either better testing the labor market or in shortening the process. Until the Labor Department has completed its report of the labor certification process, we strongly recommend that the current flexible standard be continued.

On the other hand, AILA believes that in certifying occupations that are well known to be suffering shortages, labor market information could be helpful in reducing delay and the paperwork burden. Our main fear is that absent sufficient direction, changes to the present system could inadvertently result in a situation where an employer is denied a labor certification for an alien worker, while unable to recruit a U.S. worker for the specific job. That consequence would serve no one's interest.

The immigration bar is eager to support and participate in a comprehensive study of the permanent labor certification process and commends the sponsors for including this proposal in H.R. 5115.

H.R. 5115-Section 4, Visas for Spouses and Children of Legalized Aliens

AILA strongly supports the provisions of H.R. 5115 that would permit the spouses and minor children of legalized aliens to lawfully remain with or join their immediate family members in the United States. The availability of these additional visa numbers, not subject to "per country" limitations, would go a long way toward fulfilling the promise and the dream of those undocumented U.S. residents who came forward to benefit from the legalization program.

AILA has long urged the agency charged with the administration of these laws to exercise its existing legal authority to grant these unfortunate residents a lawful, albeit interim, status to remain with their close families in the U.S. Enactment of these provisions would ensure a permanent remedy to this problem.

H.R. 5115-Section 5, Additional Visa Numbers for Second Preference Immigrants

This provision would greatly reduce and perhaps eliminate the backlog of qualified applicants who are the spouses or unmarried sons or daughters of lawful permanent residents.

In September, 1988, visas are now available to most spouses and unmarried sons and daughters of permanent residents whose petitrions were filed on or before January 15, 1987 - almost twenty months ago. However, for nationals of the Dominican Republic, the date is April 8, 1986; for the Philippines, October 5, 1981. For Mexican nationals, second preference visas are simply "UNAVAILABLE".

The provision of these additional visas would greatly relieve these backlogs and help reduce the impact of new second preference petitions to be filed by newly legalized aliens beginning in November of this year.

H.R. 5115-Section 6, 5-Year Extension of Section 314 of the Immigration Reform and Control Act of 1986

Section 314 of the Immigration Reform and Control Act of 1986 permitted nationals of certain countries that were determined to have been "adversely affected" by the abolition in 1965 of the national origins quota laws to vie for 10,000 unrestricted visas. This new provision would make 10,000 more visas available in each of the fiscal years 1989-1993 for those who submitted applications under the 1986 enactment.

This program should help many applicants whose expectations of immigration were raised, perhaps unfairly, in 1986. On the other hand, it would also continue a pejorative association with certain specific nationalities that were perceived as the main advocates and beneficiaries of this provision.

AILA believes that national origin discrimination should not be a basis for U.S. immigration law and policy. The preferred method of increasing immigration of individuals who do not qualify for family-sponsored or employer-sponsored immigration is through a nationality-neutral system of selected independent immigraton.

COMMENTS ON THE KENNEDY-SIMPSON BILL - S. 2104

AILA has commended Senators Edward M. Kennedy and Alan K. Simpson on the significant achievement represented by their sponsorship of S. 2104, the Immigration Act of 1988, and its passage by the Senate earlier this year. We support a number of the provisions of S. 2104 and believe it is an important preliminary step toward reform of U.S. legal immigration.

S. 2104 would establish separate categories for family-sponsored immigration and employer-sponsored/independent immigration, with separate worldwide levels of annual admissions. It would establish a program by which an interagency task force annually assesses and reports to the President and Congress on the impact of immigration on a variety of social and economic factors.

The Kennedy-Simpson bill recognizes the need for and would provide for increased annual immigraton to the United States. It would also establish a system for random selection of non-sponsored, independent immigrants based on a point schedule of characteristics.

S. 2104 would also establish immigrant eligibility for job-creating entrepreneurs whose minimum $1,000,000 investment creates at least ten jobs. And, like the Rodino-Mazzoli bill, it provides for a study of the permanent labor certification process, while proposing changes in INA 212(a)(14) that might benefit U.S. workers, employers, and taxpayers.

In its final form, however, S. 2104 fails to satisfy a number of principles that we think must be fundamental to proposals to reform U.S. immigration law and policy.

First, S.2104 would place numerical restrictions on immediate relatives of U.S. citizens by placing such immigrants under an overall cap on family-sponsored immigration. Under this scheme, the number of immediate relatives admitted each year would be set-off against — and would "eat into" — the number of visas available for other family-sponsored immigrants. As noted above, this historic change in our approach to and valuation of family-sponsored immigration is not justified.

In addition to this overall set-off of immediate relatives against other family-sponsored immigrants, S. 2104 would also impose a new, and lower "per country" ceiling on family-sponsored immigration. In FY 1986, the "per country" limitation on family-sponsored immigration under S. 2104 would have been 15,157, which is several thousand fewer than the actual family-sponsored immigration for each of the "oversubscribed" countries.

Further, S. 2104 would effectively lower a given country's family immigration ceiling by reducing from that ceiling the number of immediate relatives by which that country exceeded the greater of the "per country" family ceiling in the prior year or the number of "such immigrants" in FY 1988 or 1989. This reduction of family immigrants could take away up to one-half of the "per country" limit.

This complicated formula is best understood by way of the following example, which assumes "such immigrants" refers to immediate relatives and which substitutes FY 1985 and 1986 for FY 1989 and 1990 respectively. The number of immediate relatives from Mexico in FY 1986 (45,950) exceeded the level of "such immigrants" in the preceding base year (39,771, greater than the "per country" family ceiling .15,157- by 6,179). Thus, in the following year under S. 2104, Mexico's FY 1987 family-sponsored immigrants - other than immediate relatives - would be limited to 9,321 (the FY 1987 limit of 15,500 minus 6,179). In actuality, 17,119 family-sponsored immigrants were admitted from Mexico, all within its overall 20,000 "per country" limit. If, on the other hand, "such immigrants" refers to family connection immigrants, Mexico's FY 1987 limit would be about 7,750.

S. 2104 would also substantially change the current preference categories by eliminating portions of both family-sponsored and employer-sponsored categories. Under the bill's second preference category, unmarried sons and daughters 26 years old or who turn 26 before a visa becomes available, could no longer immigrate to join their lawful permanent resident parents. Under the bill's fifth preference category, brothers and sisters of U.S. citizens would lose all immigration eligibility if they marry. And, under the bill's sixth preference category, unskilled workers and skilled workers whose occupations are deemed to require less than two years training or experience would no longer qualify, despite the proven unavailability of qualified U.S. workers.

S. 2104 could also be expected to reduce overall employer-sponsored immigration due to the division of the present third preference category between the new second and third "independent" categories. Although the quota is kept about the same for exceptional ability/professionals categories, removal of bachelors degree professionals to the lower group would result in about 10,000 or more unused visas a year. Because these visas would "spill down" not to the transferred professionals but rather to the non-sponsored independent immigrant category, net, annual employer-sponsored immigration could decrease by more than 10,000 immigrants. As a further consequence, the backlogs and waiting time for skilled workers and professionals would probably increase.

Almost all of the increase in legal immigraton under S. 2104 would go to the non-sponsored, independent category, which is set at 55,000 admissions per year and could, through "spill down", exceed 75,000 annually. In our opinion, this diversion of new admissions to the non-sponsored category - while eliminating several family-sponsored and employer-sponsored preferences - is a step in the wrong direction. Increases in immigration need to be balanced, permitting experimentation with non-sponsored, independent immigration, while still affirming major commitment to family unification and sponsored immigration.

Again, AILA strongly supports the gathering and analysis of immigration facts and consequences. However, we oppose statutory provisions that could lead to an automatic or mechanical change in immigration levels or preferences. Although S. 2104 limits its automatic reduction/increase to five percent, its circumvention of the legislative process makes it, in the final analysis, inadequate to ensure the national interest.

CONCLUSION

The American Immigration Lawyers Association again commends the sponsors, Chairmen Rodino and Mazzoli and Senators Kennedy and Simpson, for initiating discussion and debate over reform of U.S. immigration law and policy.

The Kennedy-Simpson bill, S. 2104, contains thoughtful and innovative proposals that provide a useful first step in beginning to address modern reform. Many of its provisions are important improvements that should be enacted. However, S. 2104 is seriously flawed. Its inclusion of immediate relatives under a cap that eats into other family-sponsored categories, its unjustified elimination of several family- and employer-sponsored categories, and its substantial shift toward experimental non-sponsored, independent immigration should preclude its endorsement by the House of Representatives.

The Rodino-Mazzoli bill, H.R. 5115, on the other hand, is consistent with virtually all of the principles that should guide reform of legal immigration law and policy. With the minor improvements suggested above, H.R. 5115 would provide needed relief for some of the most acute immigration problems faced today by U.S. family and employer sponsors. Its trial of the non-sponsored, independent immigrant category will provide useful lessons on how well this method of immigration selection serves the needs and interests of our nation.

FOOTNOTES

[1] This text is part of Leiden's statement before the Subcommittee on Immigration, Refugees and International Law, Committee on the Judiciary, U.S. House of Representatives.

12

Past and Present Trends in Legal Immigration to the United States

JOHN M. GOERING
Commission for the Study of International Migration and Cooperative Economic Development

THESE remarks center on the system of preferences controlling legal immigration and in particular on the preference for brothers and sisters. This preference category — the fifth — is currently one of the lightening rods around which proponents and antagonists have assembled some of the latest proposals for the reform of legal immigration, namely S.2104, "The Immigration Act of 1988" and a draft "Legal Immigration Reform Plan" prepared by INS. [1]

My intention in these comments is not to celebrate either my prescience or the relevance of social science research, but rather to deplore the thin strands of evidence which currently provide the basis for policy relevant research assessments of immigration reform proposals. This is an effort to highlight some of the errors, short-sightedness, and needless contention which emerge when policy makers are unable to obtain or agree on basic facts.

A BACKWARD LOOK: BRIEFLY REVISITING THE 1952 AND 1965 REFORMS

Briefly revisiting the intentions and provisions associated with the legislative reform of immigration policy of 1952 and 1965 helps in understanding the extent to which current legislative choices represent a dramatically different or predictably similar response to the strengths and shortcomings of existing immigration law and the flow of immigrants.[2] Such a retrospective look at Congressional foresight also serves as a cautionary tale as present-day reformers attempt to peer into the future.

Such a legislative assessment recently lead Senator DeConcini to complain on the floor of the Senate that the pending legislative proposal, S.2104, constituted "an unwise step away from the traditional importance we Americans have placed upon family reunification as a cornerstone of our national immigration policy" (*CR* S.2211; March 15, l988). There are a half-dozen brief comments which emerge from an historical assessment of legislative reforms which bear on this observation and the current policy debate on the reform of the system of numerical limits and preferences.

1. Prior to 1965, the highest priority and largest proportion of visas under U.S. immigration law were allocated for labor entrants rather than for family members. Within the earlier national origins systems, 50 percent of visas went for labor purposes.

2. The "traditional" high level of importance assigned to siblings was only established in 1965 as a substitute measure of the House Subcommittee No. 1, on Immigration. The Chairman of that Committee, Congressman Feighan, introduced a fifth preference allocation for brothers and sisters of 24 percent; an action which soon resulted in labeling the amendments the "brothers and sisters act"(Reimers 1985).

Presidents Kennedy and Johnson had recommended retaining the high priority on labor visas in their legislative proposals in 1963 and 1964. Prior to this time, siblings were either in a non-prefereence category up to 1952, or were 50 percent of unused visas.

3. The preference proportions established in 1965 were subject to little Congressional assessment or debate, with the bulk of legislator's attention focused on eliminating the national origins system. Many Congressional analysts believed the system of preferences would be reformed within a short time. The reforms have already, as we now know, taken nearly a quarter of a century.

4. Congress and the Administration believed that the 1965 reforms would both have little effect on the stock of immigrants entering the United States and would eliminate backlogs. Senator Edward Kennedy (1966:145), for example, writing soon after passage of the bill argued:

> Arguments against the bill were chiefly based on unsubstanti-
> ated fears that the bill would greatly increase annual immigration,
> would contribute to increased unemployment and relief rolls...
> and would permit the excessive entry of persons from Africa and
> Asia.

Total legal immigration has of course increased mainly due to unforeseen increases in the numbers of exempt immediate relatives. Few immigrants from Africa have arrived but immigration from Asia and Latin America increased sharply since 1965. Congress was unable to anticipate that Asian immigration would increase by roughly 40 percent between 1965 and the end of the 1970s (Reimers 1985:243).

In addition, instead of zeroing out backlogs, there was a backlog of nearly 200,000 applications in fifth preference by 1968 as well as backlogs for labor visas. Abba Schwartz (1968:131), a major executive branch architect of the 1965 reforms, remarked, three years after enactment of the law: "Obviously, the distribution of the preference system was a haphazard determination which will plague the administrators of the system and the Congress with backlogs and problems until a remedy is found."

5. The Select Commission on Immigration (SCIRP 1981) did not provide recommendations on precise proportions to be allocated to preference categories for all brothers and sisters (Fuchs 1983:77). The Commission staff report, however, reflected significant disagreement with this conclusion, stating (SCIRP 1981:362-363):

> The staff believe it was undesirable to include a category with the potential for enormous, unmanageable backlogs when there was little hope of issuing visas to applicants in it. Although the staff recognized the close relationship often shared by siblings, this need was not generally believed to be as compelling as that of reuniting husbands, wives, sons and daughters. Further, the staff found that the inclusion of a preference for all brothers and sisters of adult U.S. citizens creates exponential visa demand. Married siblings — which account for about half of those entering — bring spouses who, upon naturalization, can then petition to bring their parents and siblings, along with their families. And so the chain continues.

The staff, like the Chairman of the Commission, believed that an explosive process of chain migration was swamping the country with unintended entrants. The research basis for this important judgment will be assessed below.

6. Lastly, the use of a point system which has been introduced in current legislative proposals to regulate or qualify immigrants for entry to the United States was judged to be administratively impractical by the Select Commission. Concerns about litigation over executive branch decision-making were part of the reason for not recommending the imposition of a more qualitative system for regulating admissions. The current adoption of such qualifying points reflects a recent Congressional, or political, consensus that their time has come. The research basis for assessing their use and benefits will be addressed in the following section.

RESEARCH CONCERNS

The issue of the "explosiveness" of immigrant admissions as well as concern over growing immigrant backlogs are issues which continue to involve legislative policy makers. The apparent "explosion" of chains of migrants is a politically potent metaphor whose evidentiary basis has only recently been assessed. It, therefore, seems appropriate and useful to take a moment to learn whether recent research can help illuminate the debate over these issues.

1. The Explosiveness of Immigrant Admissions
The staff of the Select Commission as well as its Chairman, Fr. Hesburgh,

hypothesized that the admission of one legal immigrant would quickly lead to the admission of up to 84 additional migrants in "runaway" or explosive additions. No research basis existed to justify this number, however. Senior officials at INS, however, currently repeat such estimates, arguing that up to 90 immigrants are spawned by one admission. On the floor of the Senate, the ranking minority member of the Subcommittee on Immigration argued on March 14, 1988, that one of the problems with the existing fifth preference is that it allows one person to bring in "64 derivative relatives on one U.S. citizenship" and, he added, "I do not think that is what we had in mind when we were talking about immediate family and family reunification." As he said:

> I do not think anyone envisioned (in 1965) that someone would bring in 64 derivative relatives on one U.S. citizenship, and when they come they come under the fifth preference. So we make a mistake of granting this extraordinary preference to brothers-in-law, sisters-in-law, and nieces and nephews of U.S. citizens. As you can see the visa demand in that category (fifth) is simply geometric. (CRS.2124; March 14, 1988).

Three recent research projects have directly addressed the issue of whether and to what degree there is an explosion of subsequent chain migrants. The research has, through a variety of methodologies, sought to determine how many relatives enter through which visa categories, over what length of time, and for what reasons in response to the admission of an initial immigrant. Two former research members of the Select Commission (Jasso and Rosenzweig 1986) have, for example, used INS and census data to construct a fairly sophisticated demographic model of the chain of immigrant admissions, naturalization, and subsequent sponsorship of relatives. This research found a multiplier in the first ten years of approximately one, with the highest rates of sponsorship from those entering under labor visas. The researchers, who had expected to find evidence of a large multiplier, indicate that fifth preference provides for the admission of 30 to 40 percent of the admissions from initial labor entrants.

A second research effort on the opinions of roughly 2,000 prospective immigrants in Manila and Seoul found that although each visa registrant had up to 25 potentially eligible relatives that only 20 to 25 percent were actually likely to emigrate to the United States. The remainder were either excludable, already subject to another petition, or did not intend to emigrate (Arnold 1987:28-29). The author's remark that "it is evident that much of the potential for the future immigration of siblings attributable to the 1986 cohort of immigrants is illusory" (Arnold 1987:29).

Finally, GAO (1988) released a report in January 1988 which also found little evidence of a multiplier, except for Asian countries. In China, for example, there was a pattern of rapid naturalization and petitioning unlike other countries where the average time between the arrival of a petitioner and his or her relatives was over 12 years. It was over eight years before naturalization occured. The study also found that "less than 10 percent of naturalized petitioners were admitted through the fifth preference category." (GAO 1988:56).

There is, therefore, at present no sound social science evidence that warrants significant political or legislative concern over an explosive multiplication of chains of migrants. Due to extensive backlogs in countries with high demand most "multiplication" is likely to occur over a twenty to thirty year period, and ten only after most applicants age considerably, with attendant diminishment of their migration aspirations. To the extent that this creeping multiplication occurs, fifth preference appears to be responsible for moderate proportions of overall chaining.

2. Backlogs of Immigrants

A second major sore spot in the current debate over the 1965 amendments is that they have generated huge, unfair backlogs of applicants. This issue appears especially acute as it bears on the admission of siblings. Senator DeConcini, for example, stated on the floor of the Senate in March 1988 that the proposed changes in fifth preference, including grandfathering, make "an intolerably long backlog for fifth preference visas even longer." The recent proposal, "Legal Immigration Reform Plan," prepared by INS also indicates a deep concern with backlogs, arguing that its provisions will "eliminate inordinate delays" and indeed within seven or eight years eliminate all backlogs. Data on the size and characteristics of the waiting list for entry into the United States help shed light on the "intolerable" nature of such visa backlogs.

Waiting lists, it appears, are neither uniform, permanent, nor well understood. In terms of their uniformity, ten countries, as of 1986, held 73 percent of the total fifth preference backlog of 1.2 million people; and indeed 38 percent was assigned to three countries: the Philippines, India and Korea. As of January 1988, the fifth preference backlog grew to 1.4 million of which 37 percent was allocated to these three countries. If Mexico is added, the percentage of the total fifth preference backlog allocated to these four countries is nearly 50 percent (47%) or 658,602 applicants. For all visa categories, the above four countries represented 51 percent of the total applicant backlog of 2.19 million registrants.

A second fact of interest is that a modest proportion of visa registrants appear to reject their visa openings when offered. In 1982, for example, 24 percent of fifth preference visa applicants became inactive and, in 1986, 14 percent, or 205,000 visas were not used. The no-show rate was much higher in certain countries with an 87 percent no-show rate for Italy in 1982 and 77 percent in 1986. In Greece in 1986 the inactive rate was 57 percent and 40 percent in Egypt. The inactive rate in China, however, was only eight percent, five percent for Hong Kong, nine percent in India, and four percent for the Philippines. For 1987 the no-show rate was 22.8 percent worldwide, and fourteen percent for fifth preference. The inactive rate in fifth preference for Italy was 82 percent, 57.5 percent in Greece, 6.7 percent in Mexico, 4.9 percent in the Philippines and 36 percent for Ireland or (1,054 out of 2,916).[3]

One of the consequences of long waiting lines is, therefore, that a small to modest proportion drop-off the list before their number is called. Another related feature is that visa registrants age as they wait with fifth preference admissions from many countries being 40 years of age or more. In the Philippines and China they are 46 to 47 years of age. As applicants wait and age, they are also more likely to become married, with 77 percent of sibling admissions being married. These proportions also appear to be increasing with entrants from China increasing their marriage rate from 73 percent to 91 percent from 1979 to 1985. Such high rates of marriage mean that a legislative provision limiting sibling admissions to only never married persons will disproportionately affect certain Asian and European countries while having less of an impact in Mexico and other Latin American countries where applicants are younger and more likely to be unmarried.

Long waiting times and levels of inactive applications may also result in, or reflect, increased levels of illegal entry; applicants may have already entered the United States. Currently, there is no means of determining what proportion of non-immigrant visa holders, or undocumented entrants, already have a petition filed for them. The absence of such data make it hazardous to conclude that applicants on waiting lists are either passively waiting their turn or have decided to enter the U.S. by any means possible while awaiting their call for a visa number.

How aggressive or passive the waiting list is, is one part of the issue of how "fair"or dangerous it is to allow applicants to wait ten to twenty or more years before being able to reunite with earlier arrivals. Considerable political and emotional force is attached to debates on the nature of the Congressional commitments to visa holders when the last visas "contract" was approved in 1965. Selective levels of inactivity suggest, but do not definitively prove, that not all visa applicants wish or need to honor their part of the contract. The effects of aging, changing economic and political conditions in sending countries, the fortunes or relatives within the U.S. economy, and the initial strength of family ties are all factors for which we lack comprehensive or even very good selective evidence (Jasso and Rosenzweig 1988).

Backlogs may, therefore, be viewed with impunity in either one or two ways: first; backlogs may be seen as a queue of close family members eager to be reunited with absent relatives under almost any condition as a line of individuals, of uncertain length, who have taken out an insurance policy of a visa petition which they may or may not use depending upon circumstances in the sending and host countries at the time their number is called. Such applicants may be indifferent to the timing of the arrival of the petition, may have alternative petitions working, may seek temporary or more permanent non-immigrant entry, or may seek entry to a third country.

A final issue that is important to address is the improbable expectation that the United States can ever issue sufficient visas to satisfy world-wide demand. Demand for such visas is generated in large measure by factors outside of the U.S. control, except insofar as severe economic recession — as in the Depression — results in a decline in immigrants' willingness to emigrate. It is also reasonable to expect that the creation of new visa categories, or opportunities, will generate heightened interest by additional categories of prospective migrants and their families. It is, therefore, a reasonable supposition — and research hypothesis — that U.S. immigration law will always stimulate more applicants than visa openings and that the length of this backlog will vary depending on push and pull factors substantially outside the control of U.S. policy makers.

SUPPLEMENTARY THOUGHTS AND NEEDED RESEARCH

A number of summary thoughts come to mind after reviewing the above scattered points of evidence. The first observation is that neither the legislative reforms in 1952 or 1965 worked entirely as their crafters intended. Quotas were systematically circumvented by the early 1960s following the 1952 reforms and family reunification has become paralyzingly slow after 1965 reformers elected to foster prompt reunification.

Second, due to the admission of derivative and accompanying relatives, the proportion of visas allocated for family reunification is close to 90 or 95 percent, with only a handful of visas used to sponsor labor entrants (Jasso and Rosenzweig 1988:V-1). [4]

Third, although Congress has waited a long time to reform the system of preferences, the work of the Select Commission has provided a measure of political legitimacy and balance which has facilitated legislative adjustments. The absence of a detailed social history of the internal operations and deliberations of the Commission means that neglected or poorly researched issues, staff-Commissioner conflicts, and omissions are not well understood.

Immigration policy making has been called "a puzzle wrapped in cliches;" political cliches among the foremost (Fuchs 1983:58). Perhaps the fact that several Commissioners joined and departed the Select Commission with their pre-judgments intact suggests that political rather than research concerns occasionally dominated their deliberations. The tendency for Congressional policy makers and others to sprinkle holy water from the Select Commission's fount is, then often all too selective; highlighting areas of agreement but ignoring areas of contention and omission.

Fourth, the breath of fresh air which will come from the required reporting under IRCA as well as the substantial reporting requirements in S.2104 are legislative choices which reflect a degree of openness and flexibility which was lost from sight in the 1965 reforms. Reports on labor market and demographic impacts, including reports on "other economic and domestic conditions" could provide the basis for more sustained , credible research on immigrant admissions and adjustment (Warren 1987). The importance of gathering such basic data and research evidence was pointed out in 1985 by the National Academy of Sciences (Levine, Hill and Warren 1985) and by Michael Teitlebaum (1980:33) who commented:

> Since the available evidence on the consequences of current immigration is weak each advocacy group is able to find some form of nominally 'scientific' corroboration for its own posture... In such a setting, it is difficult indeed for the disinterested and concerned observer to distinguish truth from misrepresentation, and to assess the merits of alternative policy approaches.

More recently, Doris Meisner (Meisner and Papademetriou 1988:104) reiterated this concern commenting that:"Without a well-funded and effective immigrant data management system, the controversy surrounding "numbers" will continue well beyond the end of the (IRCA) legalization program."[5]

It is of concern that, for the last four fiscal years, the Statistics Division at INS has received a budget of only roughly one million dollars a year to cover staffing and contract research expenses. It has had no commensurate increase in staffing in recent years despite substantially increased reporting and research requirements established by Congress.

Fifth, one of the areas where the absence of useful data and research is most apparent is in assessing the probable impacts of alternative systems of points for the admission of independent immigrants. In the rush to embrace the use of points for the selection of certain immigrants there has been a lack of assessment of the pros, cons, and tradeoffs among the various systems of points being recommended. The fact that Canada and Australia administer their point systems under quite a different system for immigrant admissions has been noted by others. The Senate Subcommittee on Immigration is, to great advantage, seeking the advice of experts on the quantitative impacts of their overall legislative proposal. This assessment, however, does not include the point system. Due to the absence of a research data base on the characteristics of immigrants and the foreign born that is suitable for such an evaluation, the point system remains an area in need of significant additional research. The partial assessment of S.2104, currently being conducted by GAO, will nevertheless offer unique insights on probable tradeoffs and impacts of the proposed preference structure.

Sixth, increases in the number of immediate relatives admitted into the United States has been one reason for the proposal to put a ceiling or cap on legal admissions. The depletion of origin-country parents, children, and siblings in Europe appears to be part of the explanation for the shifting increase in admissions and applicants from Asia and Latin America. The admission of parents of citizens as immediate relatives does not, however, appear to lead to large levels of chaining or backlogs. Research by GAO (1988a) and by Jasso and Rosenzweig (1988) indicates that one major source of this growth is from parents of citizens. Jasso and Rosenzweig (1988:V-4) note that: "the increase after 1971... would appear to reflect sponsorship or parents by newly naturalized citizens, whose own immigration became possible only in 1965."

The naturalization rates for parents of U.S. citizens is, however, only sixteen percent for women and twelve percent for men in the 1971 cohort of immigrants (Jasso and Rosenzweig 1988:II-12). [6] It is consequently unclear, and a matter in need of research, whether the current seven percent annual increase in the number of immediate relatives is likely to be sustained or whether there is a tapping-out or depletion that is likely to occur from current sending countries just as it has for European countries (Vialet 1988a:11).

The seventh and last issue of concern is the intermingling of political and nativist concerns over how many immigrants of what sort the United States should accept. Various legislative approaches to this issue are undoubtedly possible but one recent proposal had encountered considerable criticism. In introducing an earlier version of the current Kennedy-Simpson bill, Senator Kennedy (1987), for example, noted:

> I am particularly concerned about how we can...re-open our doors to potential immigrants who are unable to benefit from current immigration law. It is a question of how we correct an expected imbalance stemming from the 1965 Act — the inadvertent restriction on immigration from the 'old seed' sources of our heritage.

The criticism of this proposal, that it smacked of racism and was "unwise and dangerous" (Vialet 1988:b) quickly lead to a revamping of priority points assigned to countries 'adversely impacted' by the 1965 reforms.

There is, however, a harsher more strident facet of the concern over increasing the flow from European countries and concomitantly reducing it from Asia and Latin America. It resurrects the sounds of restrictionism that were dominant in the report of the Dillingham Commission, in 1911, on immigration. That report was straightforward in concluding that new immigrants "were different from old immigrants and less capable of becoming good Americans" (Fuchs 1983:65). As a result, that Commission recommended the continuation of the exclusion of Chinese, the restriction of Korean and Japanese immigration, and the use of a literacy test to screen out undesirables. These recommendations were enacted into law and lasted until 1952;

it was not until 1965 that special provisions restricting persons of Asian ancestry were eliminated.

These seemingly pariah — ancient — concerns over America's ethnic heritage have nevertheless achieved a more current voice and some popularity. In part because of the decline in population growth in the native American population, a growth rate below replacement, concern has been expressed over newcomers who are sharply different from the indigenous population. Teitelbaum and Winter (1985:176-178), in their assessment of this issue report one solution proposed in 1982:

> It is with grave concern that we observe the infiltration of the (German) nation by millionfold waves of foreigners and their families, the infiltration of our language, our culture, and our national characteristics by foreign influences... The integration of large masses of (non-German) foreigners and the preservation of our nation thus cannot be achieved simultaneously; it will lead to the well-known ethnic catastrophes of multicultural societies... For the (Federal) Republic (of Germany), which is one of the most heavily populated countries of the world, the return of the foreigners to their native lands will provide ecological as well as social relief.

This statement is from the Heidelberg Manifesto written by a group of German academics concerned about rising numbers of Algerians, Turks and other putatively unassimilable ethnics. [7] Concern over similar groups in France has given impetus to the Conservative Party of Jacques Le Pen.

The United States has been spared most of these political extremes. There, nevertheless, remains a legitimate concern with understanding the limits of the absorptive capacity of the country. Senator Alan Simpson, for example, in his commentary on the final report of the Select Commission remarks: "Immigrants can still greatly benefit America, but only if they are limited to an appropriate number and selected within that number on the basis of traits that would truly benefit America." He then went on to state:

> If immigration is continued at a high level and yet a substantial portion of the newcomers and their descendants do not assimilate, they may create in America some of the same social, political and economic problems which existed in the country which they have chosen to depart. Furthermore, as previously mentioned, a community with a large number of immigrants who do not assimilate will to some degree seem unfamiliar to longtime residents. Finally, if linguistic and cultural separatism rise above a certain level, the unity and political stability of the nation will in time be seriously eroded. (Simpson 1981:413).

Concerns over the growth of linguistic and cultural ghettos are not, of course, new (Fuchs 1984; Lamm and Imhoff 1985). A recent study by the University of California, for example, documents the passage of legislation in Wisconsin which established English as the official language for public and private schools. The legislation was enacted in 1889 against German immigrants, suggesting that there may well be periods of time during which the absorption of an immigrant group will appear "too slow" (Documenting English 1987).

Understanding the rate and evenness of the social, economic, and political absorption of immigrants is frustrated by the absence of any government policy, research, or planning mechanism to address these issues. Once admitted, there is a *laissez faire* approach to subsequent adjustment issues with a concomitant disregard for systematic research on the similarities, differences, and conflicts among immigrant groups at various stages of assimilation. The evidence which exists is partial and subject to differing interpretations (GAO 1988(b).[8] Immigrants, for example may or may not have adverse impacts on labor markets. Certain immigrant groups may be assimilating residentially more rapidly than American blacks but may be retaining ethnic enclaves for temporary or permanent sanctuary (Massey and Denton 1987). The attitudes and prejudices of immigrants may come to resemble those of American minority groups which are experiencing racial and ethnic discrimination, therefore, putting them on a "par" with other "outsider" groups (Portes and Bach 1985; Gardner 1985).

Does such a maturing of an immigrant cohort represent a less than ideal absorption of values or a realistic transfer of American values and prejudices?[9] Are immigrants likely to be as "loyal" to the United States as other minorities or citizens and how do we test such loyalty to be sure it is robust? How are problems in short-term job or wage displacement balanced against evidence of the longer-term development of entrepreneurial skills and investment? How different is the economic and social adjustment of immigrants admitted for purposes of faily reunification compared to "independent" or new seed immigrants in their short- and long-term contributions. These, and a myriad of other, concerns fascinate and plague policymakers and researchers as they periodically revisit the question of how many foreigners of what sort to admit into the United States (FAIR 1988; Center for Migration Studies 1988). Re-opening the door to increased labor migration, with or without qualifying points, may do a great deal to assure front-end control of the immigration process, but indifference to the "back-end" process of absorption is needless blindsighting at a time when issues of immigrant's economic and cultural contributions is of such central significance.

The debate over how many immigrants, from which countries, the United States should select can be easily confounded by nativist concerns unless there is evidence to address the worst fears and policy speculations. Opening the door to a technical adjustment to remedy an apparent imbalance in old seed immigrants could, therefore, release a flood-tide of resentments, fears, and interest group claims which could easily suffocate the best intentioned reform proposals.[10] It is not that there is no means to put the evil genie of nativist and racist concerns back in the bottle, it is simply that the cost could be so high that the 1965 amendments would appear an ideal remedy. Without clearer, more comprehensive evidence on the economic, cultural, and political adjustment and absorption of aliens, immigration policymaking operates in partial darkness; in a vacuum created in part by legislative unwillingness to address the mechanisms of immigrant assimilation.

There has been, at least up to 1986, an indifference to the impacts of social and economic conditions upon immigrant absorption (Barker 1988) as well as limited concern about the impact of various immigrant populations upon the fabric and content of U.S. society. The significant increase in information generated by the reports required under IRCA and those established by the Kennedy-Simpson bill can — if funded and conducted rigorously — make the next round of debate over the reform of immigration policy a more creative, incremental process. Such evidence can make it easier to understand how many immigrants the United States can absorb, at what rate and to what degree, their embededeness in our social institutions, and the extent to which immigration policy needs to be made more sensitive to short- and longer-term impacts.

FOOTNOTES

The author would like to thank a number of people for assisting in gathering the data used in this analysis and, then, in making some sense of it. My deep gratitude to Michael Teitelbaum, Joyce Vialet, Dick Day, Jerry Tinker, Heather Hodges, Carl Hampe, Seton Stapleton, Bob Warren, Lisa Roney, Mike Hoefer and Dan Fabillon. I have been offered much sound advice and valuable insights. All of the narrow-sightedness and limitations are mine alone. Also, the opinions in this article do not reflect the views of the Commission for the Study of International Migration or the Federal Government.

1   This presentation and assessment assumes that there will be a degree of familiarity with current legislative proposals involving changes to the system of preferences for the admission of legal immigrants; see Vialet 1988a, 1988b.

2   For greater detail on these historical reforms see Goering (1987) and Vialet 1988c, and the detailed sources cited therein.

3   The Bureau of Consular Affairs at the State Department has recently initiated a project aimed at purging inactive files from their consular posts. This effort, designed to reduce the excess paper storage, will have the effect of either one-time increases in the use of "old" visa numbers or a permanent reduction in the level of "inactivity". The uneven nature of such purging at consular posts means that future users of data on visa inactivity cannot assume comparability with the current statistics.

It is of interest to note that the NP-5 program established under IRCA has had 15,000 registrants for 10,00 visas. Thus, 33 percent of registrants failed to appear for their visas. Some of these no-show applicants indicated to the State Department that they had changed their minds, obtained a preference system visa, or were too old.

[4] Jasso and Rosenzweig (1988 V:1) report that "95 percent of immigrants qualify under current law on the basis of their familiar relationship to another immigrant or to a U.S. citizen."

[5] Meisner and Papademetriou (1988:XVI) also state: "The critical data necessary for policy decisions have not been available. Yet, there has been a peculiar but consistent failure by INS to incorporate the data that are available in the planning of the legalization program."

IRCA's reporting requirements complement those established in S.2104 in requiring a triennial assessment of the impact of immigrant admissions on the 'economy, labor and housing markets, the educational system, social services, foreign policy, environmental quality and resources, the rate size and distribution of population growth in the United States, and the impact on specific States and local governments of high rates of immigration resettlement." Title IV of IRCA, "Reports to Congress" P.L. 99-603.

[6] Jasso and Rosenzweig (1988:II-12) go on to report that refugee men have the highest rate of naturalization of 60 percent. Spouses of citizens have a rate of 37 percent for women and 34 percent for men. The rate for labor certified immigrants is the highest in all the categories reaching 60 percent while that for siblings is less than 30 percent. Eastern Hemisphere immigrants have substantially higher rates of naturalization than those from the Western Hemisphere.

[7] Earlier, Teitelbaum (1980:57) argued that "in the long-term, it will be important to ensure that no single national, ethnic, religious, racial or linguistic group comes permanently to dominate American immigration." See also Espenshade 1986; Jasso 1988.

[8] Data (INS 1988) on the occupational status of aliens who have recently legalized, under IRCA, indicate a fair degree of heterogeneity with immigrants from Asian countries having much higher proportions of professional workers than those from Latin America. These data indicate that 26.2% of Philipinos, 33.4% of Koreans, 26.7% of Indians, and 17% of Chinese aliens who legalized held professional or executive positions. Only 2.4% of aliens from Mexico, 4% from El Salvador, and 5.7% from the Dominican Republic were also highly skilled. Of the 477 aliens from Ireland, 16.3% were highly skilled.

[9] Research by the Justice Group (1988) indicates that among the reasons people give for not legalizing are factors related to their absorption and naturalization potential. Out of nearly 500 interviews done in October 1987, 17% said they planned to return to their native country, 16% felt it would be disloyal to legalize, 16% feared a loss of native culture and 14% feared loss of their native citizenship. These percentage groupings undoubtedly overlap, suggesting a core group of 15% to 25% whose sense of national origins is a counterweight to the economic or social benefits associated with residence in the U.S. This unsystematic research is now being complemented with detailed investigations on the adjustment to and impacts of IRCA, See, for example, North (1987); Meisner and Papademetrious (1988); Cornelius (1988); Anderson (1988).

[10] See, for example, the "Statement on Legal Immigration Reform," presented at the House Hearing on Legal Immigration Legislation by the Irish Immigration Reform Movement; House Subcommittee on Immigration, Refugees, and International Law. Washington, DC, June 21, 1988.

REFERENCES

Anderson, P.
1988 "The New U.S. Immigration Law: Its Impact on Jamaicans at Home and Abroad". (January). Center for Immigration Policy and Refugee Assistance. Washington, D.C.: Georgetown University.

Arnold, F. et al.
1987 "The Potential for Future Immigraton to the United States: A Policy Analysis for Korea and the Philippines". (July). Honolulu: East-West Center.

Barker, K.
1988 "Report Finds Schools 'Overwhelmed' by Immigrants". The Washington Post. (April 21):A19.

Center for Migration Studies.
1988   "Annual National Legal Conference on Immigration and Refugee Policy". (April 21-22).
       Washington, D.C.

Cornelius, W.
1988   "Implementation and Impacts of the U.S. Immigration Reform and Control Act of 1986:
       A Comparative Study of Mexican and Asian Immigrants, Their Employers, and Sending
       Communities". Progress Report. La Jolla, CA: Center for U.S./Mexican Studies, Univer-
       sity of California.

"Documenting English - Only Movements in the U.S."
1987   UC Mexico News. No. 21 (Fall-Winter):6.

Espenshade, T.
1986   "Why the United States Needs Immigrants". PDS-86-2. Washington, D.C.: The Urban
       Institute.

FAIR
1988   "The Purpose of Legal Immigration in the 1990's and Beyond". Annual Conference (June
       10). Washington, D.C.

Fuchs, L.
1983   "Immigration Reform in 1911 and 1981: The Role of Select Commissions". *Journal of
       American Ethnic History.* 3 (Fall):58-89.

GAO
1988a "Immigration: The Future Flow of Legal Immigration to the United States". (January).
       GAO/PEMD-88-7. Washington, D.C.: GAO.

_____

1988b "Illegal Aliens: Influence of Illegal Workers on Wages and Working Conditions of Legal
       Workers". (March). GAO/PEMD-88-13BR. Washington, D.C.: GAO.

Gardner, R., B. Robey, and P. Smith
1985   "Asian Americans: Growth, Change and Diversity". *Population Bulletin.* 40
       (October):1.43.

Goering, J.
1987   "Legal Immigration to the United States: A Demographic Analysis of Fifth Preference
       Visa Admissions". Staff Report. Subcommittee on Immigration and Refugee Affairs.
       (April). Washington, D.C.: GPO.

INS
1988   "Provisional Legalization Application Statistics". Statistical Analysis Branch. Washing-
       ton, D.C.: INS.

Jasso, G.
1988   "Whom Shall We Welcome? Elite Judgements of the Criteria for the Selection of Immi-
       grants". *American Sociological Review* (forthcoming).

Jasso, G. and M. Rosenzweig
1986   "Family Reunification and the Immigration Multiplier: U.S. Immigration Law, Origin
       Country Conditions, and the Reproduction of Immigrants". *Demography.* 23 (August):
       291-311.

_____

1988   *Immigrants in the United States.* New York: Russell Sage Foundation (forthcoming).

Justice Group.
1988   "Phase III Advertising Summary". Unpublished report. (February 23).

Kennedy, E.
1966   "The Immigration Act of 1965". *The Annals.* 367 (September):137-149.

1987 "Opening Statement of Senator Edward M. Kennedy at Hearing on Legal Immigration Reform". (October 23). Washington, D.C.: Senate Subcommittee on Immigration and Refugee Policy.

Lamm, R. and G. Imhoff
1985 *The Immigration Time Bomb*. New York: Truman Talley.

Levine, D., K. Hill and R. Warren
1985 *Immigration Statistics: A Story of Neglect*. Washington, D.C.: National Academy Press.

Massey, D. and N. Denton
1987 "Trends in the Residential Segregation of Blacks, Hispanics, and Asians: 1970-1980". *American Sociological Review*. 52 (December):802-821.

Meisner, D
1987 "Testimony Before the Senate Subcommittee on Immigration and Refugee Affairs: on S-1611". (October). Washington, D.C.: Carnegie Endowment for Peace.

Meisner, D. and D. Papademetriou
1988 *The Legalization Countdown: A Third Quarter Assessment*. Washington, D.C.: Carnegie Endowment for Peace.

North, D.
1987 "Immigration Reform in Its First Year". CIS Paper 4. Washington, D.C.: Center for Immigration Studies.

Portes, A. and R. Bach
1985 *Latin Journey*. Berkeley: University of California.

Reimers, D.
1985 *Still the Golden Door: The Third World Comes to America*. New York: Columbia University.

Schwartz, A.
1968 *The Open Society*. New York: William Morrow.

SCIRP
1981 *U.S. Immigration and the National Interest Staff Report*. Supplement to the Final Report and Recommendations. Washington, D.C.: "Policy in the United States". *Foreign Affairs*. 59 (November):21-59.

Simpson, A. K.
1981 "Statement of Commissioner Alan K. Simpson". Appendix B. Final Report of the Select Commission on Immigration and Refugee Policy. Washington, D.C.: GPO.

Teitelbaum, M.
1980 "Right Versus Right: Immigration and Refugee Policy in the United States". *Foreign Affairs*. 56 (November):21-59.

Teitelbaum, M. and J. Winter
1985. *The Fear of Population Decline*. New York: Academic Press.

Vialet, J.
1988a "Immigration: Numerical Limits and the Preference System". Issue Brief 1B88018. (March 28). Washington, D.C.: Congressional Research Service.

1988b "Comparison of the Senate Passed S.2104, The 'Immigration Act of 1988' and 'Naturalization Amendments of 198 ' with Existing Law". (March 30). CRS Report 88-267EPW. Washington, D.C.: Congressional Research Service.

1988c "U.S. Immigration Law and Policy: 1952-1986". Report for the Senate Subcommittee on Immigration and Refugee Affairs. (December). Washington, D.C.: GPO.

Warren, R.
1987   "Data on U.S. Immigrants: The 1986 Immigration Act's Effects on Collection and
        Reporting". Paper presented at the 1987 meetings of the Population Association of
        America. Chicago.

13

Immigration Reform: Too Fast For Comfort?

Milton D. Morris
Joint Center for Political Studies

Quite appropriately, this panel's focus is S2104, passed overwhelmingly by the Senate on March 15, and now before the House of Representatives. Its passage is remarkable in at least three respects: 1) it is the result of an unlikely alliance — between conservative Republican Senator Allan Simpson and liberal Democratic Senator Edward Kennedy who have heretofore been far apart on most immigration policy issues; 2) it occurred with unprecedented speed and only minimal public hearings (in fact, none at all on the Simpson-Kennedy bill approved by the Senate); 3) it occurred with the knowledge of only the most attentive observers of the Senate and of immigration issues. This sharp break with the tradition of intense debate and slow decision-making that has characterized immigration legislation, occurred in the absence of any apparent pressure for swift reform of legal immigration. In considering the results of this unusual occurrence, I will focus on a few of the more noteworthy changes it contemplates as well as on some questions about the timing of the effort and the degree to which its central features are justified by the country's experience or its projected needs with respect to immigration.

As the panelists note, two basic concerns were central to the reform effort. One, stressed by Senator Simpson, is the desire to improve a firm ceiling on total legal immigration. The other, championed by Senator Kennedy is a desire to encourage more immigration from Europe or "old seed immigration". Both objectives go to the heart of the country's approach to immigration, involving changes in the annual ceiling and in the way admissions are allocated under that ceiling.

S2104 establishes a ceiling of 590,000 immigrants annually. This is approximately 100,000 more than the current level of annual legal immigration. Most analysts and policymakers seem agreed that increased legal immigration is desirable and so will find the increase welcome. However, there has been considerable, longstanding disagreement about how much immigration should be allowed or what criteria should be used in deciding on the level of immigration. S2104 involved no serious effort to consider appropriate levels or criteria for setting levels. Instead, it seems to have reached an arbitrary decision based largely on the number now coming.

Is an arbitrary decision on this important issue adequate? Does the bill assume a significant reduction in illegal immigration as a result of the Immigration Reform and Control Act of 1987? Does the bill reflect adequate consideration of current and projected labor market needs, attention to the needs of major source countries, or recent demographic projections about the country's population growth and labor market needs? This segment of the bill benefits from a provision requiring annual assessment of the social and economic effects of immigration and adjustment of the immigration ceilings at three-year intervals. However, even these measures, might not compensate for the failure to specify criteria for setting immigration levels.

A second major feature of the immigration bill is that it increases the number of independent immigrants admitted, i.e. those admitted without ties to relatives residing in the U.S., to 150,000. Of this increased number, about a third will be admitted under a new point system which ranks applicants on the basis of criteria such as education, English language ability, age, and skill levels.

The increase in the number of independent immigrants admitted, and the point system adopted, are prompted by a desire to increase immigration from Europe, and particularly from Ireland. The bill assumes that immigration from some European countries is low because the family reunification emphasis in current law discriminates against them. However, the country's immigration experience suggests otherwise. The family reunification emphasis initially favored Europeans and the 1965 amendments to the immigration law equalized entry opportunities for all countries. The decline in European immigration appeared to have had much more to do with expanding economic opportunities in those countries than with any particular feature of immigration law. One of the basic lessons of the country's efforts to control the flow of immigration is that it responds more to external economic forces than to the preferences of U.S. policymakers.

Whatever the motives for seeking to increase European immigration, it is unlikely that the bill will succeed. What we know of the dynamics of migration suggests that people migrate when they perceive economic opportunities as significantly greater elsewhere than at home. In recent years the gap in economic opportunities between the U.S. and Europe has declined dramatically or disappeared altogether. Even in the less developed European countries like Ireland, the gap is probably not large enough to constitute a powerful push force. Moreover, it is much closer to labor markets on the continent where incomes are likely to be comparable to those in the U.S.

Even if the new point system does not accomplish the intended objective of increasing European immigration, it represents a significant modification of the emphasis on family reunification as the objective of immigration policy. The 55,000 immigrants to be admitted under the point system clearly will be selected to meet perceived labor market needs. Moreover, those immigrants will enter the country equipped to compete for professional and skilled positions rather than the blue collar occupations with which most immigrants have usually begun. Some analysts, noting the country's growing demand for highly educated workers, applaud this step. However, neither the panelists here nor the bill's sponsors commented on whether this might have the effect of discouraging efforts to expand educational opportunities to those Americans who are for a variety of reasons now deprived of such opportunities.

The bill breaks new ground in its provision for the admission of up to 2000 investor immigrants each year. These are immigrants who would enter on condition that they invest $1 million as business operators employing at least ten individuals full time. As one of the few features of the bill to receive spirited debate in the Senate, it raises some important issues that might have usefully engaged the panel more than it did. While job creation is commendable and desirable, there is something deeply troubling about literally selling entry to the U.S. for a fixed price — $1 million and ten jobs. This concern, raised by Senator Dale Bumpers, was quickly dismissed by the Bill's sponsors, but has not been thoughtfully or adequately addressed by the Bill's sponsors or by the panelists.

These major new elements in immigration policy clearly require serious national debate. But even more important, the Bill has not had the benefit of the country's initial experience with the first phases of the recently enacted Immigration Reform and Control Act. Whether a firm ceiling of 590,000 immigrants is appropriate or not might very well depend on whether the new law manages to stem the flow of illegal immigration. To date, we have no idea. Several witnesses before Senate hearings on the two bills out of which S2104 emerged warned of this haste to legislate before the country has had time to evaluate the effects of IRCA and before the immigration bureaucracy had had time to fully gear up to implement IRCA.

It is ironic that after years of lamenting the difficulty that policymakers have had in making decisions about immigration policy and the very long time required to arrive at relatively simple decisions, several highly regarded immigration experts expressed serious reservations about the prudence of the rush to enact further reforms at this time. Reform is desirable, but not urgent. There are important issues that require greater deliberation than they appear to have received and some vital data are not yet in. I must conclude, therefore, that passage of S2104 is indeed too fast for comfort.

PART IV

REFUGEES

14

International Assistance to Refugees

AMBASSADOR JONATHAN MOORE
U.S. Coordinator for Refugee Affairs

MY topic is resource shortfalls in international assistance to refugees in place, and my thesis is that the privileged world is not doing enough, and that over the longer term we will have to do more.

With the proper attention being given to admissions ceilings and numbers, the need to take stock of and give priority to resources for assistance is equally if not more critical. We are now pursuing emergency consultations to get current ceilings raised and to protect admissions from Southeast Asia — continuation of strong levels of resettlement for Indochinese refugees as part of our on-going efforts to sustain first asylum has been repeatedly reasserted by various officials of this Administration.

We resettle refugees in our country because it responds to the desperate humanitarian needs of the human beings concerned, because of important foreign policy reasons, and because they enrich our society.

Thus, the State Department spends one third of its refugee budget on admissions, even though roughly 99 percent of the world's twelve million refugees will never be resettled in any third country.

While the U.S. spends $20 for each refugee in assistance contributions through multilateral organizations, who may never know living conditions above basic survival, in 1988, the federal government — including the Departments of State and Health and Human Services — is allocating nearly $6,900 in total expenditures to admit and resettle each refugee who comes to the United States.

Assistance needs for refugees immediately upon being granted first asylum and thence for maintenance in camps or settlements until longer term efforts pay off, are not now being met consistent with the aspirations of the 1951 Geneva convention on refugees or given our own national values. The *sine qua non* is for the international community to care for refugees, to keep them from being physically and spiritually burned out, in the interim. If we aren't coming up with adequate resources to do this job and yet pretend that we are, it will debase the refugees and their cause and discourage coming up with the needed funds.

Let me share with you some pictures of the dire plight facing many of the refugees in the world drawn from recent visits and daily cable traffic. In the Itang camp in southern Ethiopia there are 176,000 Sudanese who have been, without milk for months, and cooking oil for extended periods, and who were given only 1200 immunizations last year. Malawi has, in the past year and a half, received refugees from Mozambique to equal one-tenth of its own population, most of them arriving emaciated from malnutrition wearing shreds of rags; two and three of these refugees are forced to share a single hospital bed. In Pakistan, there are 150,000 tons of wheat less than what the Government of Pakistan estimates it needs to feed three million Afghan refugees, and there are also shortfalls in infant feeding supplements and in sugar and tea. In UNRWA camps in Gaza, the lack in basic sanitation encourages the spread of tuberculosis and childhood disease. In Honduras, Nicaraguan and Salvadoran refugees are confined in overcrowded camps, where water, fresh food, clothing and educational materials are in chronically short supply. In Thailand, the security abuses of Cambodian refugees in border camps demonstrates the challenges of meeting the widespread need for greater refugee protection.

In raw dollar terms, international assistance levels appear to keep pace with the enlarging refugee population. We can be grateful that total contributions to the main international refugee organizations — UNHCR, UNRWA and ICRC — have increased recently the past three years to almost $700 million annually. But the sad reality, is that the reach of these humanitarian programs is substantially less than what they assess is required, and that they inevitably set their budget levels according to the limited contributions they receive.

Under instructions from the donor community to "economize", the UNHCR has only recently issued an emergency appeal for Mozambican refugee assistance based on conservation estimates of the needy population that have already been exceeded. And the UNHCR took months to assign adequate manpower to Malawi to deal with the intense flow there because of personnel restrictions imposed on it by donor states.

This year emergency appeals from international refugee organizations are generally up. Those of the International Committee of the Red Cross alone are 46 percent above last year's appeals for ICRC's important relief and protection work in Africa, Southeast Asia, Central America, Afghanistan and the Middle East. It remains unclear how well the international community will respond to them. The U.S. response is running $4 million lower than last year, and our President's $50 million special fund to meet unpredictable emergencies is depleted to $12.6 million, without any replenishment over a two year period.

Available funds for international refugee assistance are devoted principally to basic care and maintenance projects for refugees in dire emergency situations, as they should be, while self-sufficiency, education, and developmental programs are more underfunded. For the so-called "long-stayers", endless subsistence programs do not suffice. Over time, refugees obviously need incentives and the tools with which to envision and create a future — basic education and self-sufficiency programs so they can take charge of their lives by developing the skills to set up cooperatives and agriculture extension projects, and build farm-to-market roads — all means to creating a productive existence in the camp and beyond. These needs are not being adequately met. We estimate, for example, that two-thirds of all refugee children do not have access to primary education.

Finally, if we don't make progress on root causes, on reducing the flow of refugees, we will fail in our mission. Current examples include strengthening the Orderly Departure Program given the tripling of Vietnamese boat arrivals to Thailand over the past year, and efforts to feed starving Ethiopians in their own country so they don't have to flee to Sudan. Upcoming aspirations include providing repatriation assistance in Afghanistan so the Afghan refugees in Pakistan can go home and withdrawal of the Vietnamese from Cambodia and stabilizing of conditions in that country enabling eventual return of the Khmer now in Thailand border camps. Durable solutions involve local resettlement and repatriation for refugees as well as their resettlement through admissions programs. The international community must invest more in these efforts. In some instances these initiatives will involve less financial costs than in the case of others but none can transpire without the investment of funds.

In absolute terms, the United States remains well as the forefront of overall contributors to international refugee organizations. This year the United States will spend $176.2 million in support of the refugee programs I have outlined. The next largest donor, the EEC, contributes about half of that. Yet in the short run, our national commitment to deficit reduction — fiscal limitations and the Executive-Legislative budget agreement — place real constraints on us. Our contributions this year are 9 percent under 1987 levels. The U.S. contribution to ICRC is down from 17 percent to 12 percent. Similarly, our traditional 29 percent contribution to UNHCR has dropped to 24 percent. The cut in the U.S. contribution to the UN Relief and Works Agency from $67 million to $61.3 million is also particularly wrenching in this sensitive period of events in the occupied territories.

Compared to other major donors, the U.S. ranks only eighth among the top 20 in contributions to international refugee funds when our allocations are measured on the basis of our per capita population. This is up from 12 in 1980 and down from five in 1985. Contributions from Nordic countries, consistently at the top of the list, have jumped from $2.50 to $4.32 per capita in the past three years; and EC countries among the top 20 have more than doubled their average per capita contributions to $1.50. The U.S. per capita contributions have stagnated below the level of one dollar, and with the decline of the dollar, the real value of the discrepancy between the European and U.S. contributions is even greater. And there is a strong relationship between our response and that of others. This reality was recently expressed by a foreign ministry official of another leading industrial state who noted, with regard to one of the many international refugee appeals, "The actual size of our contribution will depend on the program needs and the contribution of the US".

In summary, the world needs to provide more resources, we need to reinvigorate international burden-sharing — the contributions of other nations for assistance to refugees, along with the United States — so that a reconfirmation of this humanitarian commitment is achieved. Until we get more resources we must mobilize all those that are already available with a proper priority for assistance programs and allocate them with as much flexibility and equity as we can. And we must find a way to give higher priority to this mission to which we have long provided proud leadership.

15

Refugees and Resources [1]

GUY S. GOODWIN-GILL
Senior Legal Adviser, UNHCR, Geneva, and Law School, Carleton University

AT first blush, there might seem to be little or no connection between the concerns expressed by Ambassador Moore and those of other panelists, who have focused on the proposed new asylum regulations. In fact, that link, joining the national and international dimensions of the refugee problem, is clearly identifiable, even as it highlights limits and limitations in the existing system of protection and solutions.

Ambassador Moore mentioned the resource problems now facing nation States, international organizations and the international community at large, and resources in this context cover a broad spectrum: resettlement places for refugees for whom this solution means protection and a new life; material support for those in need of shelter, food, basic health care, education and employment; personnel who are the essential link between donors and recipients; funding, which is the means to the end; and above all, the political will without which solutions will not be forthcoming, or refugee flows averted, or claims to protection dealt with fairly and expeditiously.

More can be done, of course, but due regard must be paid to the variety and complexity of the world's involuntary migrations. A special value is rightly placed on the right of individuals to belong, to adhere to their community of origin, to return to the land of their birth. But the politics of every situation (whether the precise focus be racial, religious, economic or other) generally mean that there can be no *a priori* hierarchy of solutions. What will always be required is a sophisticated approach to each and every crisis, combining all such elements of solutions as will effectively meet humanitarian needs, produce the necessary funding, open up the possibilities of repatriation, resettlement and local integration, and ensure the provision of protection.

Protection means ensuring the fundamental human rights of refugees and asylum-seekers while simultaneously assisting actively in the development and implementation of answers.

The existing international system of protection has evolved over the last sixty years, and has proven valuable as an effective mechanism for the resolution of refugee problems and the defense of refugee rights. It was always an incomplete system, however, and current pressures are opening fissures which, in the past, tended to be overlooked. For example, many hundreds of individuals continue to leave Vietnam by boat. Only a very small percentage are found to be motivated by a well-founded fear of per secution, to have had any connection with the pre-1975 authorities in the south, or to be members of particular ethnic minorities. Once outside their country of origin, however, they cannot return or be returned; their humanitarian needs may be further compounded by the trauma of their flight, by the brutality of pirate attacks and push-offs. Since 1979 the international system (States and organizations) has been unable to deal with this group as other than refugees for whom the single solution of resettlement must be found.

In Europe, a number of measures have been taken in recent years to curb the numbers of those arriving to claim asylum. In a continent where regular immigration opportunities are practically non-existent, the refugee status procedure is an attractive alternative, appearing to offer admission and the assurance of security, welfare and education. It naturally draws those in need of protection, who have a well-founded fear of persecution or other valid reasons for flight, such as intercommunal violence or international conflict. Among those arriving will also be those who are seeking greater security or opportunities than are available in countries of first refuge, as well as others who are not refugees, but are motivated solely by economic reasons or considerations of personal convenience. The European response has included an extenson of visa requirements, sanctions for airline companies which transport insufficiently documented passengers, stricter interpretation of refugee criteria, and resistance to the claims of those whose needs might fall outside the provisions of the 1951 Convention/1967 Protocol Relating to the Status of Refugees.

Today's problems are by no means limited to these two regions. In other parts of the world, refugees and asylum-seekers may be detained, or denièd access to procedures, or *refouled* or they may suffer serious discrimination and treatment intended to coerce their 'voluntary' return.

All of the above problems are necessarily affected by resource shortfalls and a lack of political will; they are accentuated by organizational and juridical deficiencies. For example, the Office of the United Nations High Commissioner for Refugees has been set the complementary objectives of providing international protection and seeking permanent solutions. By the terms of its Statute, however, it remains a reactive organization, passively awaiting the next cross-border flow before it may contemplate action or response. UNHCR has no competence to address root causes, and its interest in causes generally seems confined to verifying the basis of claims to protection and assistance lodged by those who have already fled.

What is required are ways and means by which root causes - responsibility - can be addressed and mitigated within a non-confrontational, international environment sensitive to the sovereign sensibilities of States, but conditioned by the fundamental obligation to respect and ensure human right.

Systemic weaknesses also require to be remedied. Both protection and solutions are heavily dependent on voluntary financing, and have to be pursued within a context of sovereign entities. The existence of international legal obligations may not be denied, but it is still not clear what States should do when others breach established principles. During the first months of 1988, Thailand initiated a policy of refusing refuge to Vietnamese boat people, backed up by a practice of push-offs which resulted in considerable loss of life. Only the USA was prepared to join UNHCR protesting against this turn of events.

International law is also insufficiently developed to ensure effective protection. It allows States to resort to measures of rejection falling short of refoulement, or fails adequately to circumscribe their discretion. Because States are themselves primarily responsible for implementation of the 1951 Convention/1967 Protocol, so the notion of auto-interpretation permits restrictive application of these basic instruments, or enhances the use of discretion for purposes alien to the objectives of protection. Certain problems are inherent in the process of determining Convention refugee status itself, where the criterion of well-founded fear introduces a host of potential variables through its basis on individual credibility and the related questions of probability and prediction. The decision of the U.S. Supreme Court in INS v. Cardoza-Fonseca highlighted the place of discretion in national asylum practice. Some observers were apprehensive lest emphasis on the discretionary elements contribute to the growth of a sub-category of refugees, unable to find any durable solution to their plight. The recent ruling of the Board of Immigration in Pula heralds a welcome change of direction, in large measure confirmed by the proposed new asylum regulations published on 6 April 1988.

International law in fact says little about the procedural details, although the minimum requirements can be read back from the provisions of the 1951 Convention/1967 Protocol, from the principle of non-refoulement and the objectives of protection and solutions. Standards deriving from the field of fundamental human rights will also regulate treatment, promote individual dignity and integrity, and even confirm the minimum basis for a hearing and appeal or review.

The new asylum regulations will constitute a considered part of the system of international protection. They reflect one State's perception of the role which national procedures have to play, but are nonetheless welcome for their effort to offer a structured approach, within the limits of the legislative framework, to dealing with the problems of elucidating facts, events and apprehensions, and determining whether a well-founded fear of persecution exists. All who have had to decide such matters, whatever the context, will know how hard it is, and how often it seems to get harder with experience. Concrete proof is rarely attainable; there is no limit to the amount of resources which might be thrown at the process, or how widely the search for evidence and documentation might be extended. In practice resources are not infinite; a line has to be drawn, and decision-makers have to be content with less. Here, practice, training and sensitisation to the plight of the refugee often can bridge the gap, while alternatives to the luxury of case by case determination might be both efficacious and responsive to national concerns (for example, by recognizing that presumptions favourable to particular groups may be raised by the cumulative effect of testimony and other evidence, subject to rebuttal where grounds are established which place the individual beyond any entitlement to protection).

The system of protection is a remarkable achievement, both in its national and international dimensions. It will remain so and develop, however, only if the resources are forthcoming, if notions of burden-sharing and solidarity are re-invigorated, and if the essential political will to address refugee problems on a humanitarian level can be exploited within and between nation States.

FOOTNOTES

1   The views expressed are the personal views of the author and are not necessarily shared by the United Nations or the Office of the United Nations High Commissioner for Refugees.

16

New Asylum Rules: The Need for Reform in Asylum and Refugee Protection in the United States

ARTHUR C. HELTON

Director of the Political Asylum Project, Lawyers Committee for Human Rights, New York, New York

EIGHT years after the passage of the Refugee Act of 1980, its mandate that uniform and neutral standards be utilized in conferring refugee protection remains unfulfilled. Rather, the Act's mandate is subservient to foreign and domestic policy considerations which continue to dominate protection determinations. In practice, refugees fleeing communist-dominated regimes have traditionally been favored over those fleeing other repressive and authoritarian regimes. Differential treatment and unfairness also occurs in the application of the standards for refugee recognition, with some asylum seekers facing virtually insurmountable burdens of proof

Proposed Regulations

Against the background and tradition of implementation problems under the Refugee Act, on April 6, 1988, revised proposed asylum regulations were published in the Federal Register.[1] Rules were originally proposed on August 28, 1987.[2] Under the August 28 version, the immigration judges of the Justice Department's Executive Office for Immigration Review were no longer to have jurisdiction over asylum and witholding requests. Instead, these functions were to be performed exclusively by "Asylum Officers", employees of the Immigration and Naturalization Service (INS), who were to render decisions in "non-adversarial proceedings".[3]

The plan to oust immigration judges from the asylum adjudication procedure, however, engendered considerable controversy.[4] As a consequence, the Department of Justice announced on December 10, 1987, its intention to modify the rule to provide for continued jurisdiction by immigration judges over asylum or withholding requests presented by aliens in exclusion or deportation proceedings. [5] The modified rule, re-published in the Federal

In Defense of the Alien

Register, provided for public comments by May 6, 1988.[6] No final rule has yet been issued.

The April proposal contained several improvements, including strengthened confidentiality for asylum claims (particularly in deportation proceedings;[7] use of international standards to determine refugee status and benefits (including authorization to work while a claim is pending);[8] use of liberal protection criteria for those who have suffered persecution in the past and who have left countries in violation of an exit visa requirement;[9] use of a narrower definition of when a refugee should be denied protection because he or she has resettled elsewhere;[10] establishment of a procedure requiring that crewmen and stowaways be removed from their "conveyances" to have their claims determined;[11] and the establishment of a corps of professional, specially-trained asylum adjudicators responsible to a central authority, who are to receive training from outside the Immigration and Naturalization Service.[12]

However, comprehensive rule-making was delayed and, on July 27, 1988, the Justice Department proposed in the Federal Register a discrete amendment to current asylum procedure.[13] This revision was similar to a component of the April 6 proposal, and would permit U.S. immigration judges to limit the scope of evidentiary hearings on certain asylum claims. Public comment on the proposal was to be provided by August 26, 1988.[14] As of yet, there is no final rule.

RECOMMENDATIONS

The need for reform in U.S. refugee adjudication, however, goes well beyond the need for improved final asylum rules. Following are recommendations for reform which might serve as an agenda for discussion of appropriate policy in the next Administration.

1. In terms of refugee doctrine, the United States departs from the international regime in one important respect — the imposition of an overly restrictive strandard of proof on refugees who seek to avoid return (refoulement) to a territory where they may face persecution. The U.S. requires proof of a "probability" of persecution, while international law requires but proof of a "well-founded" fear of persecution. This divergence should be addressed by amending domestic law (Section 243(h) of the Immigration and Nationality Act, as amended) to substitute the term "refugee" for "alien," thereby incorporating the international standard into the domestic witholding of deportation provision.

2. Since 1980, the U.S. has operated under interim regulations that provide insufficient safeguards against improper political influence in asylum and refugee admissions determinations. Criteria for refugee recognition should be set forth fully in regulations to guide adjudicators and provide notice to asylum and refugee applicants. Guidelines and instructions for adjudicators should be comprehensive, continuously updated and made readily available to the public.

3. Rules should also be issued to strengthen confidentiality for asylum claims (particularly in deportation proceedings); use international standards to determine refugee status and benefits (including authorization to work while a claim is pending); use liberal protection criteria for those who have suffered persecution in the past and who have left countries in violation of an exit visa requirement; use a narrower definition of when a refugee should be denied protection because he or she has "resettled" elsewhere; and establish a procedure requiring that crewmen and stowaways be removed from their "conveyances" to have their claims determined. These were elements of rules proposed for public comment in April 1988, but not yet issued.

4. Some of the most serious problems in U.S. asylum and refugee protection concern implementation. For example, the State Department should not provide opinions on the ultimate question to be decided in individual asylum cases — whether the refugee has a well-founded fear of persecution. Such conclusory pronouncements simply serve to continue the ideological bias which the Refugee Act of 1980 was designed to eliminate. Should the Department wish to make information on general country conditions available to the adjudicator, then that information should be revealed as well to the refugee and his or her counsel. Only through such disclosure can proper weight be given to the position of the State Department.

5. Asylum adjudicators should be high-level professionals capable of independent assessment and judgment on fact-sensitive cases which involve complex background conditions in the country of origin. Adjudicators should be recruited generally from outside INS, to avoid the cynicism and insensitivity that may attend long service in a law enforcement function, and the attendant application of overly-restrictive criteria. Adjudicators should be instructed in the law and history of human rights and refugees and be exposed to different perspectives through creative in-service training programs. This ongoing training should involve groups such as the office of the United Nations High Commissioner for Refugees (UNHCR), the international organization charged with supervising the compliance of state parties to the Protocol, as well as non-governmental advocates of the rights of refugees.

6. Traditionally, immigration judges have come from the ranks of the INS. Judges inculcated with the law enforcement ethos of the INS are sometimes incapable of giving a refugee the benefit of the doubt in the presentation of an asylum claim. The members of the administrative tribunals which hear asylum cases, including on appeal, should be organized into separate subgroups or tribunal "parts" and recruited generally from outside the INS.

7. The quality of the processing of refugee claims from abroad must also be improved. Recruitment, training and in-service instruction should be the same for refugee admissions adjudicators as for asylum adjudicators. Also, the procedures by which such claims are examined must be improved to

accord with notions of basic due process of law. Adverse decisions should be in writing and give reasons for the denial of refugee status so that meaningful reconsideration or appeal can be sought by an applicant. There should be a right to an administrative appeal from an adverse decison, and a right to judicial review under appropriate circumstances. Cases decided previously under flawed criteria or procedures should be reviewed by the authorities as a matter of course. Only with such changes can the processing of refugee cases abroad be made fair and humane.

8. More fundamentally, after eight years of flawed implementation, the function of asylum and refugee adjudication should be removed from INS. The enforcement function of the agency is incompatible with a sensitive examination of refugee claims. The protection function should be lodged in a separate agency, even a new office within the Department of Justice.

9. The opportunity should be maintained for a full due process hearing for asylum applicants who are inititally denied recognition as refugees. The recent consensus on continuing the role of immigration judges in asylum adjudication recogizes the grave interests at risk for the individual — life or liberty. The need for procedural due process is paramount under these circumstances.

10. One desirable structural safeguard in the review of refugee determinations is formal involvement in the process by the United Nations High Commissioner for Refugees. Such a role would help depoliticize the process. The role of the UNHCR in the determination of refugee status varies from country to country. A formal role for the UNHCR in the United States would assist in rationalizing the adjudication system.

11. Alien interdiction and detention programs violate the rights of asylum seekers. The focus of reform should not be on deterrence, which is designed to either encourage refugees to return to or stay in their home countries and run the risk of persecution, or to have them go elsewhere and shift the burden to other countries of asylum. Rather, the focus should be on establishing a fair asylum adjudication system. Resources should be committed at a sufficient level to ensure that adjudications are expeditious, without compromising basic dur process. Deterrence measures like interdiction or detention should be ended by the U.S. and, when followed by other governments, condemned by the U.S.

12. A formal safe haven policy should be established for those individuals in the United States who would not be protected by a generous interpretation of the "refugee" definition, but who nonetheless should not be forced to return to their home countries (e.g., victims of natural disaster, innocent civilians caught in the crossfire of a civil war, etc.). The first groups to receive temporary protection under the policy should be those who have fled the civil wars in El Salvador and Nicaragua.

CONCLUSION

Despite the enactment of the Refugee Act of 1980 the integrity of asylum and refugee protection in the United States is threatened. The Act continues to be subverted through the legally questionable practices of interdiction, detention and unfairness in adjudication. Full and fair implementation of the Refugee Act requires the depoliticization of the asylum and refugee admissions process, the recognition of the uniform Protocol standard, a serious commitment of resources and, above all, the acknowledgment of the minimal individual rights and dignity of asylum seekers. Only then will the promise of the Refugee Act be fulfilled.

FOOTNOTES

[1] 53 Fed. Reg. 11,300-10 (April 6, 1988). Adjudicators have been operating under interim rules (45. Fed. Reg. 37,392-96 (June 2, 1980)), which were finalized in only one respect in 1983, as they pertain to the allocation of jurisdiction between a district director and immigration judge to decide an asylum request (48 Fed. Reg. 5,885 (Feb. 9, 1983)).

[2] 52 Fed. Reg. 32,552-61 (Aug. 28, 1987). See Helton, *Asylum Rules Revisited: An Analysis*, 65 Interpreter Releases 367-73 (April 11, 1988); Helton, The proposed asylum Rules; An Analysis, 64 *Interpreter Releases* 1070-80 (Sept. 21, 1987). 32,556 (Aug. 28, 1987).

[3] See proposed 8 C.F.R. Section 208.8 (a), 52 Fed. Reg. 32,556 9Aug. 28, 1987).

[4] Los Angeles Times, Oct. 15, 1987, Part I, p. 1, col. 5; National Law Journal, Sept. 21, 1987, at 3, col. 1.

[5] 52 Fed. Reg. 46,776 (Dec. 10, 1987). See also Los Angeles Times, Oct. 28, 1987, Part I, p. 3, col. 2; Washington Post, Oct. 30, 1987, at A23, col. 1; Interpreter Releases 1214-15 (Nov. 2, 1987).

[6] 53 Fed. Reg. 11,300 (April 6, 1988).

[7] Proposed 8 C.F.R. Section 208.6, 53 Fed. Reg. 11,304 (April 6, 1988).

[8] Proposed 8 C.F.R. Sections 208.7 and 208.13, 53 Fed. Reg. 11,305 and 6 (April 6, 1988).

[9] Proposed 8 C.F.R. Section 208.13 (b) (2) (ii), 53 Fed. Reg. 11,306 (April 6, 1988).

[10] Proposed 8 C.F.R. Section 208.15, 53 Fed. Reg. 11,306 (April 6, 1988).

[11] Proposed 8 C.F.R. Section 253.1, 53 Fed. Reg. 11,310 (April 6, 1988).

[12] Proposed 8 C.F.R. Section 208.1, 53 Fed. REg. 11,303 (April 6, 1988).13. Proposed 8 C.F.R. Section 208.10, 53 Fed. Reg. 28,231-33. (July 27, 1988).14. Id. at 28,231.

[13] Proposed 8 C.F.R. Section 208.10, 53 Fed. Reg. 28,231-33. (July 27, 1988).

[14] Id. at 28,231.

17

INS. v. Cardoza-Fonseca, One Year Later: Discretion, Credibility and Political Opinion

DEBORAH ANKER
Lecturer on Law Fieldwork Clinical Instructor Harvard Law School

THIS presentation discusses some interesting and, in some respects, surprising developments in asylum decision making at the Board of Immigration Appeals ("BIA" or "Board")[1] since the issuance of the Supreme Court's opinion in *INS v. Cardoza-Fonseca* [2] just over one year ago. In*Cardoza-Fonseca* the Court held that the burden of proof in asylum cases[3] was "well-founded fear" of persecution, a standard distinctly different and more generous than the "clear probability" standard that had been imposed by the Board of Immigration Appeals.[4] The decision was hailed by some members of the immigration bar as well as civil rights and human rights groups as tremendously significant. It not only appeared to ease the burden for asylum claimants but, in finding that both statutory language and international law constrained administrative action, the decision represented a rare assertion of judicial authority in the immigration area.[5]

It was not at all clear, however, that the Court's ruling would result in a more generous asylum policy (The Executive Office of Immigration Review does not publish statistics on the outcomes of asylum decisions and so perhaps the most telling evidence is unavailable). Following the Court's decision, some experienced immigration practitioners as well as government officials predicted that a major effect of the Court's liberalization of the standard of proof would be an increased emphasis on the credibility determination[6] (an area over which courts have traditionally deferred to administrative and other first-tier decison makers) and on discretionary denials for those who had established eligibility of asylum under the well-founded fear standard. A focus on credibility and discretionary based denials in asylum cases seemed both presaged or at least permissible under the Court's holding in *Cardoza-Fonseca* , and consistent with trends in Board decison making before the *Cardoza-Fonseca* opinion was issued.[8] Both credibility and discretionary based denials would result in decisions turning, to a large extent, on issues tangential to the underlying claim of persecution. In the case of credibility based rulings, the applicant's testimony could be dismissed as generally untrustworthy and unbelievable and therefore no substantive inquiry would be necessary into the merits of the claim. As to discretion, a claim could be denied either despite the establishment of a well-founded fear, or irrespective of it.[9]

Instead, the aftermath of the Supreme Court's ruling is a reversal of the pre-*Cardoza-Fonseca* trend at the Board relying on credibility and discretionary based grounds for denial. In a major turnaround, the Board significantly limited the scope of discretion in asylum cases. Although the Board has continued to emphasize the importance of the credibility determination, the Board has shifted the focus to credibility problems that are both major and central to the applicant's claims. Indeed, fewer decisions may rest exclusively — or explicitly — on an assessment of the applicant's credibility. Instead, the Board, has utilized another basis for denying many asylum claims: a narrowing conception of persecution and political opinion under the statute. Although denial on the merits is hardly new, [10] it has been more frequently relied upon and more fully elaborated in recent cases. This position may once again, as in *Cardoza-Fonseca*, bring the Board into conflict with the federal courts, or more particularly with the Ninth Circuit court of appeals, which has taken a very different view, interpreting the statutory terminology to accommodate the context of current political conflicts in Central American and Caribbean nations.

DISCRETIONARY DENIAL: A NEW EMPHASIS ON BALANCING AND AN AFFIRMATIVE PRESUMPTION

Before *Cardoza-Fonseca* was decided, the Board had issued a number of precedent decisons which had the effect of making most misrepresentations in the entry process by an asylum applicant a very strong negative discretionary factor weighing heavily towards denial of asylum as a matter of discretion.[11] Use of a false passport to gain airline passage, or misrepresentations to U.S. officials to gain access to the United States and the asylum process were virtually *per se* bases for denial of asylum as a matter of discretion, even where the applicant established a "clear probability" of persecution for purposes of obtaining withholding of deportation relief under section 243(h) of the Act.[12] The Board also viewed any contact, no matter how minimal, that the applicant had with a third country as a discretionary basis for denial of asylum. Rather than enter or attempt to enter the United States, the Board effectively held that most asylum applicants could or should use the overseas U.S. refugee admissions process and be subject to the numerical and nationality limitations of those programs. Indeed, in unpublished decisons, the Board seemed to be holding that any irregularity in the manner of entry of an asylum applicant — including entry without authorized status, use of a smuggler (a factor inevitably associated with most Central American claims), or "avoidance" of the overseas process (even where, as in Central America, there was no program for overseas admission) — created a presumption of denial on discretionary grounds.[13] The effect of this trend potentially could have been denial of asylum in virtually every case.

This trend appears to have been substantially modified with the Board's decision this past fall in *Matter of Pula*[14] In that case the Board held that the applicant's use of a false passport was only one factor to be weighed in the discretionary balance. The Board also found that in making the discretionary determination, the adjudicator must consider the quality of the applicant's contact and status in any third country through which he travelled or in which he resided before coming to the United States to apply for asylum. Most importantly, *Pula* effectively reversed the negative presumption of earlier caselaw. Rather than its earlier position that any misrepresentation created a presumption of denial, the Board in *Pula* effectively adopted an affirmative presumption, holding that "the danger of persecution should generally outweigh all but the most egregious of adverse factors".[15] This position had been advocated in federal court, before the Board and in various public policy fora.[16] Although *Pula* certainly does leave room for future discretionary denials based on the applicant's manner of entering the United States, it is no longer a possibility that any manner of entry issue in an applicant's case can provide the basis for a discretionary denial.[17]

CREDIBILITY. A NEW FOCUS

The Board's post-*Cardoza* view of the credibility determination clearly also has changed, but that change, although significant, is far less dramatic than is the Board's reassessment in *Pula* of the discretionary aspect of asylum. Unlike discretion, after *Cardoz-Fonseca* credibility remains an important basis for denial, but the focus and emphasis upon the credibility determination has shifted. That change in the Board's view of the credibility determination is consistent in some important respects with the Board's new stance on discretionary denial.

A critical question underlying the credibility determination in asylum cases is how to evaluate and what weight to give an applicant's own testimony where it is essentially the only evidence produced in support of the persecution claim.[18] Before *Cardoza-Fonseca* was decided, the Board already had suggested that an applicant's own testimony might be sufficient to sustain an asylum claim.[19] In *Matter of Mogharrabi*[20], the Board's first precedent decision following *Cardoza-Fonseca*, the Board seemed to lay to rest any lingering notion that an applicant's uncorroborated testimony can be dismissed as inherently self-serving. In *Mogharrabi* the Board reiterated the Supreme Court's conclusion that the asylum statute "obvious[ly] focus[es] on the individual's subjective beliefs in assessing whether a fear is well-founded".[21] The Court's emphasis on subjective fear and on the relative generosity of the asylum statute creates some presumption in favor of giving the applicant's testimony the benefit of the doubt. Although the Board did not go this far, in *Mogharrabi it did for the first time clearly hold that*

[T]he lack of [corroborative] evidence will not necessarily be fatal to the application. *The alien's own testimony may in some cases be the only evidence available, and it can suffice where the testimony is believable, consistent, and sufficiently detailed to provide a plausible and coherent account of the basis for his fear*[22]

The impact of *Cardoza-Fonseca* is evident from a comparison of unpublished credibility rulings at the Board in 1985 with a sampling of those issued in 1987 after the Supreme Court's decision was issued.[23] A 1985 study of unpublished Board asylum and withholding of deportation decisions concluded that "throughout the unpublished caselaw, considerations peripheral to the alien's testimony regarding the persecution claim itself are factored into the credibility determination".[24] For example, in 1985 Board decisions, a widely cited reason for negative credibility findings was the same factor that counted against the applicant on discretion. The Board considered the applicant's lies to INS officials or commission of some misrepresentation in the entry process as evidence that she had "little regard for the truth"[25] and therefore her testimony as to the merits of the persecution claim largely could be discounted. In contrast, "past dishonesty" was not a significant credibility factor in any of the 1987 cases reviewed. Instead, inconsistencies between the testimony was the major credibility related reason for denials in the sample of post-Cardoza 1987 cases.[26] Moreover, whereas earlier cases had focused on inconsistencies that were often peripheral to the applicant's claim, the 1987 caselaw has held at least in principle that "trivial"inconsistencies in the alien's testimony, unrelated to her "overall claim of persecution", are insufficient to discredit her otherwise "detailed, believable account of events".[27]

Although the major change in the Board's view of credibility is a shift away from past dishonesty to testimonial and other discrepancies and inconsistencies, to some extent the Board has de-emphasized credibility more generally. Fewer Board decisions seem to rely exclusively on a negative credibility assessment.[28] Indeed, the Board recently has held that an immigration judge need not make an explicit credibility ruling.[29] This does not mean that credibility will cease to be an important element in asylum decision making. Rather, an assessment of credibility may become an implicit rather than. stated basis for negative rulings. This possibility raises serious problems, particularly since cultural misunderstandings and translation errors can have a critical impact on the credibility determination.[30] These are the kinds of factors that are too easily hidden in the adjudicatory process.

NARROWING CONCEPTION OF THE MEANING OF PERSECUTION AND POLITICAL OPINION

Rather than discretion and credibility, in recent months the Board instead has based most denials on a narrowing interpretation of the meaning of political opinion and persecution under the Act. In defining these terms the Board has focused upon individual actions and motivations sometimes in isolation from the context in which they occur.[31] With increasing determination the Board is rejecting the Ninth Circuit position that political opinion can be *imputed* without any overt political activities on the part of the victim of that persecution.[32] The Ninth Circuit has held that an individual can be the victim of persecution if he chooses to remain neutral in the midst of a civil war like that in El Salvador, where each side demands affirmative action of allegiance, as long as the stance of neutrality is conscious and accompanied by specific threats or acts of violence against the individual claiming persecution.[33] The Board also appears to be rejecting the line of cases in the Ninth Circuit which holds that persecution often can be defined not by the actions or motivations of the victim, but rather by the actions of the persecutor, which, when it is a governmental authority, presumptively acts out of political motivation.[34] The Ninth Circuit's view of persecution encompasses forced recruitment by non-governmental forces. According to that court, forced recruitment is a clear deprivation of liberty and "tantamount to kidnapping".[35]

The Board instead has found that the action of either side in the Salvadoran conflict against their victims is a normal incidence of civil war, and even, in some sense, justifiable. In *Matter of Maldonaldo-Cruz*, the Board denied asylum to a Salvadoran whose claim was based on fear of both the military and the guerillas after he was forcibly recruited by the guerillas and then escaped.[36]

In *Maldonado-Cruz*, the Board did not apparently dispute the applicant's assertion that the threat to his life from the guerillas was realistic. The Board held, however that any harm he would suffer "is part of a military policy of the guerilla organization, inherent in the nature of the organization",[37] and not on account of his "imputed political opinion" or any desire on their part to persecute.[38] The Board analogized the guerillas to a country which has established rules of military conduct and has a "right... to punish those who violate them.[39] The Board went on to reason that "[t]here is an implicit presumption of a legitimate basis for punishment."[40]ql/   As to the claim that the government would persecute Maldonado-Cruz because of his unwilling involvement with the guerillas, the Board held that:

If the government of El Salvador has received information implicating the Respondent as a guerilla, then it has a legitimate right to seek him out and determine whether he is indeed involved with such an organization... If a citizen of the United States is alleged to belong to a clandestine organization which is operating in the United States and is engaged in violent activity to further its political goal, federal authorities would properly seek him out. The Government of El Salvador has a legitimate right to take similar action.[41]

As already indicated, what is most interesting, and disturbing about the Board's current view of political opinion and persecution, is its efforts to justify governmental and even guerilla repression as legitimate — or inevitable — in the context of an on-going civil war. The Board's position comes close to holding that the more pervasive the violence — and perhaps incidences of repression — within a country, the more difficult it will be to prove an individualized persecution claim. [42] At the same time, the Board defines persecution as centrally concerned with overt indicia of politically based motivations of the alleged persecutor and victim without any evaluation or judgment regarding human rights conditions in the country from which the applicant claims persecution.[43] In *Maldonado-Cruz*, the Board found that the actions of the Salvadoran government were legitimate without any ruling regarding the human rights record of the Salvadoran government and governmental military and paramilitary forces. The Board purported to make a neutral and general judgment about the legitimacy of governmental action. Yet in other contexts - Iran and Afghanistan, for example - the Board clearly has made judgments regarding the political legitimacy of particular governmental and opposition action in ruling in favor of the applicant on the merits of his persecution claim.[44] The normative political judgments that are implicit in political asylum cases might best, instead, be made openly so that the real concerns that inform political asylum decison making can be subject to public scrutiny and judicial review.[45]

FOOTNOTES

[1]   This article will make reference to decisions of the Board of Immigration Appeals which are "unpublished". Only a small proportion of the Board's decisions officially are published and designated as "precedential". *See* A. Aleinikoff and D. Martin, *Immigration: Process and Policy* 93 (1985); 8 C.F.R. sec.103.3(e).

[2]   _____ U.S. at _____, 107 S. Ct. 1207 (1987).

[3]   The Immigration and Nationality Act as amended by the Refugee Act of 1980, provides two distinct types of relief for an applicant physically present in the United States claiming persecution in her home country. Section 243(h), 8 U.S.C. sec.1253(h) (1982) provides for mandatory withholding of deportation or return from a country where an alien's "life or freedom would be threatened ... on account of race, religion, nationality, membership in a particular social group, or political opinion". The relief is limited, however. It only precludes deportation to the persecuting country, but does not prevent return to any third country nor does it confer a status in the United States. Section 208(a), 8 U.S.C. sec 1158(a) (1986) provides for a discretion—ary grant of asylum where an alien establishes a "well-founded fear of persecution on account of race, religion, nationality, membership in a particular social group, or political opinion". Although asylum is discretionary, it is a more generous form of relief than withholding, not only, as the Supreme Court held, in terms of the eligibility standard but also in that it confers a status in the United States which can eventually lead to permanent residency. For a more complete discussion *see* Anker "Discretionary Asylum: A Protection Remedy for Refugees Under the Refugee Act of 1980" 28 *Va. J. Int'l L.* 1, 1-6 (1987).

[4] The Court earlier had upheld the probability standard as appropriate in 243(h) applications in *INS v. Stevic*, 467 U.S. 407 (1984).

[5] The plenary power of the political branches over immigration, resulting in extreme judicial deference and often extending to actions and determinatons of administrative officials, has been the subject of a great deal of analysis and criticism. *See e.g.* Legomsky, *Immigration Law and the Principle of Plenary Congressional Power, 1984 S. Ct. Rev. 12.* The court's relatively non-deferential stance in *Cardoza-Fonseca* was the result of the strong Congressional policy expressed in the asylum statute, as well as the foundation of that policy in international law. The Court also was reviewing a "question of law" and a statutory eligibility requirement, not a discretionary element. In a recent case, upholding the denial of a motion to reopen in the asylum context, the Court expressed a more traditional and deferential attitude towards review of agency determinations. *INS v. Abudu*, _____ U.S. _____, 56 USLW 4195 (1988) at 4207. ("INS officials must exercise especially sensitive political functions that implicate questions of foreign relations and therefore the reasons for giving deference to agency decisions on petitions for reopening or reconsideration in other administrative contexts apply with even greater force in the INS context").

[6] Because of the pervasive difficulties of obtaining corroborative proof, the credibility determination always has been considered a critical element in persecution claims. *See e.g.* Martin "The Refugee Act of 1980: Its Past and Future" in Transnational Legal Problems of Refugees, 1982 Mich.Y.B. Int'l L. Stud. 91, 105 ("Asylum determinations..revolve critically around a determination of the applicant's credibility"); McGrath "Credibility determinations: Avoiding Adverse Findings in Asylum Hearings and Defeating Them on Appeal" 16 *Imm. Newsletter* 3 (July-August 1987); Helton, "Credibility Determinations In Asylum Cases" 4 *Feder. Immig. L. Rptr.*, No. 28, 12-18 (hereinafter "Helton I"; No. 31, 12-15 (1986) (hereinafter "Helton II"). *See Generally*, Blum, "The Ninth Circuit and the Protection of Asylum Seekers Since the Passage of the Refugee Act of 1980", 23 *San Diego L.R.* 327, 365-66 (1986). In *Cardoza-Fonseca* the Court recognized that subjective fear is an explicit and important aspect of asylum doctrine itself. In interpreting the statutory "well-founded fear" language the Court stated "[t]hat the fear must be 'well-founded' does not alter the obvious focus on the individual's subjective beliefs..." _____ U.S. _____, 107 S. Ct. 1207 at 1210 (1987). Credibility clearly is a critical element in the evaluation of subjective fear.

[7] *See* notes 2 and 3 *supra*. The Court in *Cardoza-Fonseca* discussed similarities between the grant of discretionary authority in asylum and in various forms of discretionary deportation relief where the Court generally has given broad range to the Attorney General's exercise of discretion. *See* _____ U.S. at _____, 107 S. Ct. at 1220 (1987); but *see* Anker *supra* note 3 at note 194 and accompanying text analyzing (the Court's decision as consistent with a limited conception of the role of discretion in asylum).

[8] *See generally* Anker *supra* note 3.

[9] *See e.g. Matter of Salim* 18 I. & N. Dec. 311 (BIA 1982) (denying asylum on discretionary grounds despite the fact that the applicant had established eligibility based on his persecution claim). Like asylum, most forms of discretionary relief are bifurcated with statutory eligibility requirements and a further provision for the exercise of discretion (For a discussion of other forms of discretionary relief and their relationship to asylum *see* Anker *supra* note 3 at 43-49). The alien must establish statutory eligibility without which discretion cannot be exercised. However, relief can be denied on discretionary grounds without a finding on eligibility. *See INS v. Rios-Pineda*, 471 U.S. 44, 449-50 (1985); *INS v. Bagamasbad*, 429 U.S. 24, 26 (1976) (per curiam). The Board has held that asylum can be denied in the exercise of discretion based on the applicant's conviction for certain crimes, without a hearing on eligibility and consideration of the merits of his persecution claim. *See generally* Anker *supra* note 3 at 51-54. *See also* note 11 *infra*.

[10] For example, in *Matter of Acosta*, a *pre-Cardoza-Fonseca* Board decision comprehensively dealing with a variety of issues under the asylum statute, the Board already had applied a strict interpretation to the meaning of "political opinion". [T]he requirement of 'persecution on account of political opinion' refers not to the ultimate political end that may be served by

persecution but to the belief held by an individual that causes him to be the object of the persecution". Interm Dec. No. 2986 at 26. After *Cardoza-Fonseca* was decided, the Board overruled that aspect of the *Acosta* decision equating the well-founded fear and clear probability standards, but found the general definition of persecution articulated in that decision still relevant. *Matter of Mogharrabi* Interm Dec. No. 3028 at 11 (BIA 1987).

[11] *See generally* Anker *supra* note 3 at 1-49. These "manner of entry" issues are not the only bases upon which the Board has denied asylum as a matter of discretion. The Board also has denied asylum on discretionary grounds based on the applicant's commission of certain "particularly serious" or "serious non-political crimes", or on a finding that she engaged in the "persecution of others". *See Id.* at 51-54; note 11 *supra*.

[12] *See supra* note 3.

[13] *Id.*

[14] Interim Dec. No. 3033 (BIA 1987).

[15] *Matter of Pula* Interim Dec. No. 3033 at 10 (BIA 1987). For a critique of the Board's discretionary asylum jurisprudence *see generally* Anker *supra* note 3.

[16] Id. See also, Anker Speech, Annual Capitol Conference, American Immigration Lawyers Association, November 1986, Washington, D.C. (tape available through author); Anker, Blum Comments on Proposed Asylum Regulations, October 1987 and May 1988 (available through author).

[17] For a critique of the limitations of the *Pula* decision *see generally* Anker *supra* note 3. Although the Board appears to have discounted manner of entry factors in the discretionary determination, the Board apparently has considered these same factors as a basis for denial of voluntary departure to applicants who entered the United States to seek asylum, but whose claims were denied by the Board on eligibility grounds. *See e.g. Matter of Perez-Alvarez*, A26 950 684 (BIA Sept. 30, 1987) (unpublished decision); *order affirm'd and reinstated Matter of Perez-Albarez* A26 950 684 (BIA Dec. 17, 1987) (unpublished decision) (*petition for review filed*, U.S. Court of Appeals for the First Circuit, No. 88-1105) (substaining the Service's appeal of an immigration judge's grant of voluntary departure; the appeal of the grant of voluntary departure was based on the applicant's use of a smuggler to enter the United States).

[18] It should be noted that there is an important distinction between the question of whether the testimony will satisfy the burden of proof in asylum and whether that testimony is credible and believeable. "Court opinions often confuse determinations of credibility with assessments of the burden of proof, engaging in the process of weighing the sufficiency of the proferred evidence, rather than evaluating the actual believability of the testimony". McGrath *supra* note 67 at 3.

[19] *See Matter of Acosta*, Interim Decision No. 2986 (BIA 1985), at 10. Earlier in *Matter of McMullen*, 17 I & N Dec. 542 (BIA 1980), the Board had reversed the immigration judge and found the applicant's testimony "self-serving" and hence not credible. This finding was overruled by the circuit court. *See McMullen v. INS*, 658 F.2d 1312, 1319 (9th Cir. 1981) (holding that BIA could not discredit applicant's uncontroverted testimony without at least suggesting what further evidence the Board would require). In *Acosta* the Board apparently modified its position in *McMullen* finding, that without an explicit negative credibility ruling, an immigration judge could not dismiss an applicant's testimony solely because it is "self-serving". Interim Dec. No.2986 at 10.

[20] Interim Dec. No. 3028 (BIA 1987)

[21] *Id.* at 5.

[22] *Id.* (emphasis added) at 10, The Board's solicitude for uncorroborated testimony, however, was qualified. The Board emphasized that "...every effort should be made to obtain such [corroborative] evidence" and that " 'the lack of corroborative evidence does not necessarily mean that unsupported statements must necessarily be accepted as true if they are inconsistent with the general account put forward by the applicant.' " *Id.* (citing UNHCR's *Handbook*).

[23] The pre-*Cardoza* analysis is based on a study of 1985 unpublished decisions. *See* Anker and Bernstein "Unpublished Asylum and Withholding Decisions at the Board of Immigration Appeals:1985" (hereinafter "1985 Unpublished Asylum and Withholding Decisions" (unpublished manuscript available through the author). While the 1985 study analyzed all of the asylum decisions issued by the Board that year, the post-*Cardoza* 1987 cases discussed in this article are simply a sampling of unpublished opinions decided by the Board during that period in which the credibility issue seemed to be emphasized.

[24] Anker and Bernstein "1985 Unpublished Asylum and Withholding Decisions" *supra* note 22 at 17.

[25] *Matter of Almanzar-Estrella*, A27 037 739 (BIA 12/12/85) (unpublished decision) cited in Anker and Bernstein "1985 Unpublished Asylum and Withholding Decisions" *supra* note 23.

[26] Inconsistencies and discrepancies had been a factor cited in earlier decisions as well. *See generally* McGrath *supra* note 6.

[27] *See Matter of Mohibi* A27 497 579 (BIA 7/27/87) (unpublished decision) at 5.

[28] *See e.g.*, *Matter of Trejo-Mendoza* A26 373 648 (BIA 2/19/88) (unpublished decision) (relying both on a negative credibility ruling and on a determination of the merits of the applicant's claim to deny asylum). In *Trejo-Mendoza* the Board deferred to the immigration judge's negative credibility ruling that the applicant's testimony regarding his many political activities was "suspect" *and* found that those activities and his treatment and anticipated treatment by governmental authorities did not constitute persecution on account of political opinion within the meaning of the Act.

[29] *See Matter of Vigil* Interim Dec. No.3050 at 12 (BIA 1988).

[30] *See generally*, Kalin "Troubled Communication: Cross-Cultural Misunderstandings in the Asylum Hearing"; McGrath *supra* note 6; Anker and Rubin "The Right to Adequate Translation in Asylum Proceedings" Imm. J. 10, (July-Sept. 1986).

[31] For example, in *Desir v. INS*, No. 86-2064 (9th Cir. March 7, 1988) the Board had characterized beatings, imprisonment and assault by Haitian Ton Ton Macoutes for the puposes of extortion as a personal conflict. The court overruled the Board and held that these actions did constitute persecution under the Act. "...the Haitian government under Duvalier operated as a 'kleptocracy, or government by thievery, from the highest to the lowest level. The Ton Ton Macoutes, an elaborate network of official and semi-official security forces...formed the heart of the system....Because the Macoutes are an organization created for political purposes, they bring politics to the villages of Haiti. To challenge the extortion by which the Macoutes exist, is to challenge the underpinnings of the political system." *Desir v. INS*, slip opinion at 6.

[32] *See e.g. Lazo-Majano v. INS*, 813 F.2d 1432 (9th Cir. 1987) (holding that a threat by a military leader to report the victim as subversive constituted an imputed political opinion). *But see Campos-Guardado v. INS*, 809 F.2d 285 (5th Cir. 1987) (restricting the imputed political opinion concept to "extreme" circumstances). In contrast, the Board has held that the term persecution is centrally concerned with the overt political beliefs and actions of the victim. The Board's test for persecution based on political opinion is set forth in *Matter of Acosta*, Interim Dec. No. 2986 (BIA 1985) holding the applicant's evidence must establish that 1) the alien possesses a belief or characteristic a persecutor seeks to overcome in others by means of punishment of some sort; 2) the persecutor is already aware, or could easily become aware, that the alien possesses this belief or characteristic; 3) the persecutor has the capability of punishing the alien; and 4) the persecutor has the inclination to punish the alien. *Id.* at 22.

[33] *See e.g. Bolanos-Hernandez v. INS*, 749 F.2d 1316, 1324-1325 (1984). In *Matter of Vigil*, Interim Dec. No. 3050 (BIA 1988) at 6-7 the Board criticized the implicatons of the Ninth Circuit's "'neutrality is a political opinion' series of cases."

[34] *See e.g. Hernandez-Ortiz v. INS*, 777 F.2d 509, 516 (9th Cir. 1985). ("When a government exerts its military strength against an individual or a group within its population and there is no reason to believe that the individual or group has engaged in any criminal activity or other

conduct that would provide a legitimate basis for governmental action, the most reasonable presumption is that the government's actions are politically motivated.")

[35] *Arteaga v. INS*, 836 F.2d, 1227, 1232 (9th Cir. 1988).

[36] Interim Dec. No. 3041 (BIA 1988) Maldonaldo testified that he and a friend were kidnapped by the guerillas and forced to participate in an operation against his village. His friend tried to escape and was killed. Maldonaldo-Cruz then escaped, left El Salvador, and was told while waiting for a bus to leave El Salvador, that the guerillas were looking for him. He claimed persecution by the guerillas as well as by the military forces whom, he said, would persecute him because of their "perceived political opinion" that he is a member of the guerillas. *Id.* at 4.

[37] *Id. at 11.* at 9.

[38] "The respondent's problem is not that the guerillas are motivated to hate him because of political views they 'impute' to him, but rather is that he has breached their discipline in a way that cannot remain unpunished". *Id.* at 12. The Board reasoned that "([e]ven though guerillas may have the political strategy of overthrowing the government by military means, this does not mean that they cannot have objectives within that political strategy which are attained by acts of violence, but whose motivation is not related to any desire to persecute". *Id.* at 7.

[39] *Id.* at 11.

[40] *Id.* at 12.

[41] *Id.* at 11-12.

[42] This approach of the Board was criticized by the court in *Bolanos-Hernandez v. INS*, 749 F.2d 1316, 1323 (9th Cir. 1984). "The Board's conclusion that the threat against Bolanos' life was insufficient simply because it was representative of the general level of violence in El Salvador constitutes a clear error of law....It should be obvious that the significance of a specific threat to an individual's life or freedom is not lessened by the fact that the individual resides in a country where the lives and freedom of a large number of persons is threatened. If anything...that fact may make the threat more serious or credible."

[43] *Matter of A.G.*, A26851062 (BIA 12/28/87) (designated for publication) is somewhat of an exception. There the applicant claimed conscientious reasons for not serving in the military. He testified that he considered the Salvadoran military "terrorist" and that his "moral values" prevented him from serving in an army "which has engaged in violations of human rights". *Id.* at 4. The applicant submitted extensive documentary evidence regarding human rights violations in El Salvador. *Id.* The Board dismissed this evidence (which included a statement of opinion from America's Watch) since it came from "private unofficial bodies [and] do not constitute evidence of condemnation by recognized international governmental bodies, which would be necessary at a minimum for us to accept this argument". *Id.* However, the Board's evaluation of other governments, Iran and Afghanistan, from which it has sustained some political asylum claims, has not apparently been supported by evidence in the record of condemnations by "recognized international governmental bodies". *See infra* note 43. Board member Heilman at times has made moral and political judgements about the legitimacy of particular governmental action and argued that these issues should be more explicitly addressed. In his concurring opinion in *Matter of Trejo-Mendoza*, A26373648 (BIA 2/19/88) (unpublished decision) he argued that assistance to armed rebellion is presumptively a criminal act which the government of El Salvador has the right to punish. *Id.*, concurring opinion at 3. The applicant in that case belonged to a revolutionary student group which engaged in various protests and other activities against the government. The evidence in the record indicated that the Respondent had allowed his truck to be used "to transport students to anti-government demonstration". Mr. Heilman speculated that if the respondent "in fact lent his truck to the guerillas for their use in transporting the guerillas or their supplies" there appeared to be no evidence in the records to this effect, the government had a right to punish him absent evidence that the government of El Salvador denied its citizens the right "to agitate for peaceful political change". *Id.*, concurring opinion at 4. Mr. Heilman also found that "there is no reason in this record to find that [the Respondent's] self-described 'participation in the revolutionary activities' on the level of 'passing out propaganda leaflets', should be considered activity protected under the asylum provisions". *Id.*

44   *See e.g. Matter of Mohibi*, A27497579 (BIA 7/27/87) (unpublished decision). In contrast to its decision in *AG* and *Trejos-Menjano* in *Mohibi* the Board sustained an asylum claim of an Afghan applicant based in part on his refusal to join the "Soviet controlled Afghan army" and on his participation in the Hizbeh Islami opposition movement. The Board found that there was nothing in the record to indicate that the respondent had engaged in violent acts and "[m]oreover, it is not surprising that the resistance movement of which he was a part did engage in some violence, since the aim of the resistance is to overthrow the Afghan government, and to that end, a virtual civil war has been ongoing since 1979". *Id.* at 5. The Board also found that the evidence of widespread abuses perpetrated by the Afghan government and its agents" and "[t]he overall picture...of a troubled nation engaged in civil strife...marked by endemic human rights abuses" was supportive of the applicant's individual claim. *Id.* Similarly in *Matter of Mogharrabi*, Interim Dec. No. 3028 (BIA 1987) the Board sustained an Iranian asylum claim where there was minimal individualized evidence submitted. In that case the Board recited an unusually relaxed standard for the degree of corroboration required to prove persecution by a country's government: "Where the country at issue in an asylum cases has a history of persecuting people in circumstances similar to the asylum applicant's *careful consideration* should be given to that fact in assessing the applicant's claims." (emphasis added). *Id.* at 10. Consistent with this holding, the Board in *Mogharrabi* apparently required very little, if any, affirmative proof of Iran's persecution of persons such similar to Mogharrabi. Although there was evidently no documentation of Iran's "history of persecution" in the record, the Board dismissed the question in one sentence: "The Service does not dispute that opponents of the Ayatollah Khomeini are often persecuted for their opposition." *Id.* at 14.

45   *See* Note "Political Legitimacy in the Law of Political Asylum" 99 *Harv L. Rev.* 450, 469, 471 (arguing that the normative political judgments which necessarily underlie decisions on political asylum claims be made explicit and that the requirement that an applicant demonstrate that she would be individually singled out for persecution is "indefensible").

PART V

MIGRATION POLICY:
HEALTH AND EDUCATION

18

Funding Initiatives to Improve the Health of Migrant Farmworkers: One Foundation's Story

CAROL RUTH AUSUBEL
Program Officer, Milbank Memorial Fund

ONE of the nation's oldest foundations, the Milbank Memorial Fund originally was founded as the Memorial Fund Association in 1905 by Elizabeth Milbank Anderson in honor of her parents, Jeremiah and Elizabeth Lake Milbank. Becauses of its broad charter to "improve the physical, mental and moral condition of humanity and generally to advance charitable and benevolent objects", the Association was able to support diverse humanitarian causes, including higher education for women, social welfare and public health.

Throughout the years, the Milbank Memorial Fund became involved in the local control of communicable disease, in particular, tuberculosis. It later moved on to nutrition, mental health, strengthening the medical school departments of social, community and preventive medicine in the Western Hemisphere, and studying both health needs and medical education in Latin America. Subsequently, the Fund examined issues impacting consumer utilization of health services, assisted in faculty support for East African medical schools, and sponsored a study of higher education for public health. During recent years, through its Scholar Program, the Fund provided support for training in clinical epidemiology for selected members of medical school faculties. The Milbank Memorial Fund is closely identified with *The Milbank Quarterly*, a scholarly journal which has excelled in covering matters of health policy since 1923.

In keeping with its tradition of addressing public health problems of significant need and intellectual challenge, in 1985, the Fund's Board of Directors approved a new program in occupational health. Initially, priority would be given to projects targeted to migrant farmworkers, who, as one of the nation's most exploited group of workers, lack the power to call attention to their problems. The combination of poverty, malnutrition, substandard housing, inadequate sanitation, nonexistent or unenforced standards for workplace protection and safety, and restricted access to health care virtually guarantees that migrant farmworkers and their families will suffer from poor health.

To adequately raise the health status of migrant farmworkers, we first need to better understand their problems. There is a dearth of information regarding their chief medical complaints, the nature of their illnesses, their risk of injury and disability, and the pattern of their health services utilization. Add to this the question of cost, and ready answers become all the more remote. Yet, without partial answers, it is exceedingly difficult to propose creative solutions, no less implement lasting improvements. Seeking to attract needed research in this field, the Milbank Memorial Fund supports well-designed biostatistical, epidemiological, and socioeconomic studies. We will not, however, subsidize medical care or contribute toward the construction or maintenance of health facilities; such endeavors are beyond our modest means.

Notwithstanding our genuine interest in disease and disability arising from or related to the workplace, a fine line exists between "workers" and "community" Society, therefore, must shoulder some of the social and economic burdens of illness, disability and reduced productivity. In addition to producing disease in farmworkers, working conditions such as lack of sanitation and exposure to pesticides create environmental health problems for the general population by contaminating food and polluting ground and surface-water.

The Fund decided to use two different but complementary approaches. It would award grants to institutions seeking to impact migrant health and also launch a small operating program to devleop networking and to provide technical assistance. Thus, the program objectives were:

1) to access the needs and opportunities for improving the health of migrant farmworkers;

2) To help raise public awareness of migrant farmworker problems, and to influence government, as well as the private sector, to function at higher levels of activity and effectiveness;

3) To increase communication and problem-solving among institutions presently concerned with migrant farmworkers;

4) To ensure implementation of policies and programs in occupational health by supporting both research and community efforts, and by monitoring private and public-sector initiatives.

Because of a limited amount of available funds, it was important to be selective from the start. Proposals need not only address one or more of the objectives listed above, but should appear feasible as well. Replicability is another strong selling point. Originality helps, but how many "unique" projects actually exist? And, let us not forget the applicant organization's track record, considering also the qualifications of the key people involved.

In a time of diminished and competing resources, these decisions are difficult, but necessary.

Because we are funders, and therefore, merely facilitators or catalysts, we rely on others to translate our objectives into action. Although it is tempting to accept credit for other people's effects, the praise really goes to the people who make it happen: the scientists and epidemiologists who conduct important research on the effects of pesticides; the community organizers who focus attention on right-to-know and other key issues; the farmworker groups attempting to achieve public education; and the health care workers who design innovative projects, as well as screen, treat and counsel migrant farmworkers.

It often has been a challenge to identify which worthy projects to support. A total of 38 grants have been awarded during the past three years. I believe that we have funded the best grant applications which were submitted, but is that enough? We do not solicit proposals, depending instead on interested groups to come to us with their ideas.

At the request of the Board of Directors, I recently categorized the Fund's occupational health grants, thereby creating a taxonomy of sorts. The following categories were used to classify the projects: biomedical, biostatistical, or epruction or maintenance of health facilities; such endeavors are beyond our modest means.

Notwithstanding our genuine interest in disease and disability arising from or related education, training and direct service; and dissemination, that is, conferences, publications and documentaries. I discovered that a little more than half of the nearly one million dollars awarded to date had supported research efforts, approximately twenty percent had been devoted to education and data compilation, thirteen percent each had gone to community action and health education, and the remaining three percent to dissemination.

Now, to provide you with some examples. One of the best organizations representing the interests of migrant and seasonal farmworkers is the Farmworker Justice Fund (FJF). For the past two years, we have been funding its Health Advocacy Project, which is directed by Valerie Wilk, the author of a well-known resource on farmworker occupational health. As you are well aware, FJF can report considerable progress resulting from its work in the areas of field sanitation and pesticide reform. Ron D'Aloisio already has cited some of these accomplishments, so I will say little more than that we are proud to count this group among our grantees.

Two years ago, the Milbank Memorial Fund awarded a grant to the Colorado Department of Health's Migrant Health Program to support a migrant farmworker health status survey. Those of you familiar with the Center for Migration Studies' outstanding *International Migration Review* may recall an article which appeared last Fall co-authored by Carla Littlefield and Charles Stout. Utilizing data collected in a sample survey of migrant farmworkers in Colorado to determine their health needs, health services utilization, and overall access to care, the report addressed basic issues in the funding and delivery of health care services to this population. This survey currently is being adapted by health planners across the country who wish to develop a comprehensive data base to describe their respective farmworker populations.

We also are funding a major research effort directed by Linda Rosenstock, MD, MPH, from the Harborview Occupational Medicine Program of the University of Washington at Seattle. One study will examine the effect of 1983 legislation which expanded farmworker coverage under the state's workers' compensation system. To characterize the submitted and accepted claims for work-related illnesses and injuries among farmworkers, researchers will inspect all claims filed for occupational diseases, paying close attention to pesticide-related illnesses. Another study will investigate the health effects of chronic exposure to organophosphate pesticides among apple orchard pesticide applicators.

The accomplishments of the Fair Share Research and Education Fund in Portland, Oregon illustrate the importance of developing local leadership and community action. After a long struggle, its Migrant Health Care/Pesticides project achieved the extension of a right-to-know protection for the state's farmworkers. This campaign culminated in the passage of legislation which requires agricultural employers to provide information and training in easily understood language to employees prior to their initial exposure to toxic substances. The group's current activities center on enforcement of these standards. It also will collaborate with The Work Group on Pesticide Health and Safety, a task force of Northwest community agencies which is ably coordinated by Alice Larson, PhD, to train outreach workers to educate farmworkers about pesticides and their rights under the law, to actually perform outreach and training to farmworkers, and finally, to expand clinic services for migrant and resident farmworkers.

To communicate these activities to the general public, the Milbank Memorial Fund last year provided support to the National Center for Policy Alternatives to publish and distribute a handbook on pesticide reform. More recently, the Fund awarded a grant to the Hudson River Film and Video Company to produce a documentary for national public television on the present and future of American agriculture, which will include coverage of the health of migrant farmworkers.

Because of its highly targeted approach to a very complicated problem, the Fund has had to contend with an increasingly complex set of issues. Thus, the program has widened just enough to be responsive to diverse and growing needs, without straying from its original focus. Who could have predicted, let alone prepared for, the impact of the Immigration Control and Reform Act, or of AIDS on the health of migrant farmworkers?

The Fund maintains a flexible and responsible procedure for reviewing all proposals. Grant applications are handled fairly, and there are no self-serving interests. Grants are awarded to qualified non-profit organizations to support activities falling with the Fund's stated area of interest. Bound by budgetary constraints, however, we cannot always fund everyone or to the extent that we wish.

It is a truism that any organization is only as good as its people. The Fund was fortunate in attracting a visionary president, a talented group of technical advisers, a supportive Board of Directors, and a hardworking staff. Without their invaluable assistance, this unusual program hardly could have been initiated, no less maintained. For a small, private operating foundation located at a prestigious Manhattan address to select migrant farmworkers as the source of its benevolence is most definiately not a popular choice in today's philanthropic world. I wish that other funding agencies had the courage to join us. On the other hand, there are many needy causes presently neglected.

Although foundations enjoy the supposed luxury of making key funding decisions, they continually struggle over choices which are as vital to creating or maintaining their reputations as it is to their constituents' survival. Unfortunately, there are more worthwhile projects to support than there are available resources. I will submit that grantmakers confront their share of difficulties in fulfilling a range of different roles. Just as fundraising presents uncertainties, grantmakers live in a risky world. One may argue that many of these risks are of their own creation, and that, moreover, foundations can affort to take risks. Indeed, foundations are even expected to profit from their mistakes by turning them into learning experiences.

Too often, foundations are accused of being pompous, ostensibly taking delight in refusing to bestow even a small fraction of their philanthropy upon deserving groups. Without becoming overly defensive, I would like to dispell this myth, at least as far as the Fund is concerned. Perhaps this perception of greed and power is warrented in some instances, but hopefully, not too many. Noblesse oblige may not rank as the leading trend of the eighties, but neither well-intentioned giving nor liberal idealism have gone entirely out of style.

These are weighty, but real concerns. On a daily basis, I deal with more pragmatic issues, such as getting the word out to the right people, and getting out the right word. Or certainly, as close to right as possible.

At the same time, I doubt that networking is as effective as it often is cranked up to be. Having agonized through the preparation of an annual report, I wonder whether any written product is read as carefully as intended, if at all.

This audience has listened patiently to many bleak reports on migrant farmworkers punctuated by depressing statistics and illustrated by moving anecdotes. By now, some of you must feel discouraged, others possibly outraged. The purpose of my telling you about the work going on in this field was not to paint a rosier picture of the situation than actually exists, but to encourage you to channel some of that frustration and anger into new production areas of research and assistance to this most exploited group.

19

Medical Exclusions: The Players and Policy

JOANNE LUOTO, M.D., M.P.H.
Chief, Refugee Program, U.S. Public Health Service

REFUGEE health matters are the responsibility of the Department of Health and Human Services (USDHHS) and, more specifically, the Public Health Service (PHS). Within the Public Health Service, the Office of Refugee Health (ORH) is responsible for policy and coordination activities. Accordingly, the ORH deals with refugee health and mental health policy overseas, during processing, and following resettlement in the U.S.

The U.S. Public Health Service activities relative to refugees include the following:

Consultation with the Department of State (DOS), Bureau of Migration and Refugee Affairs, with regard to overseas health and mental health diagnosis and treatment for U.S.-accepted refugees;

Consultation and classification of medical exclusion cases, and determination of eligibility for a medical waiver;

Inspection of refugee medical records at U.S. Ports of Entry;

Notification of health agencies about refugee arrivals, and follow-up of serious medical conditions;

Administration of a program for health assessment and referral for treatment of refugees following resettlement; and

Provision of policy advice to the Office of Refugee Resettlement (ORR) relative to medical and mental health services availability during resettlement.

Additionally, the ORH administers a program for medical consultation to the INS, detention and deportation, and for the provision of medical services to undocumented aliens at selected service processing center sites throughout the U.S. The ORH also coordinates the provision of mental health services to the DOJ for Cuban entrants at the INS Detention Facility at St. Elizabeth's Hospital in the District of Columbia, and oversees a DOJ outplacement residential community program for Cuban entrants.

The legal bases for medical exclusion were most recently legislated by the U.S. Congress in the Immigration and Nationalities Act of 1980 (8 U.S.C. 1101 1982). The purpose of medical exclusions is to prevent admission of those persons who "would endanger public health or safety, as well as those who would....present a social or economic burden to society." (Dr. J. E. Mason, Director, CDC, 98th Congress, 1984).

In summary, there are eight gounds for medical exclusion in that law, contained in Sections 212 (A) 1-7 and 15. Medically excludable persons include aliens who are:

1. Mentally retarded;
2. Insane;
3. Have had one or more attacks of insanity;
4. Afflicted with psychopathic personality, sexual deviation or mental defect;
5. Narcotic drug addicts or chronic alcoholics
·6. Afflicted with any dangerous contagious disease
7. Certified as having a defect, disease or disability of such a nature that it may affect the ability to earn a living;... or,
15. Likely at any time to become public charges.

As some of these terms are not consistent with current medical understanding and nomenclature, and definition of the content of some of these categories has been necessary. The Public Health Service does not classify conditions referable to sections (7) and (15); application of those two grounds remains the responsibility of the Immigration and Naturalization Service.

There is, in addition, considerable involvement of other Federal agencies in administration of medical exclusions. The Department of State has responsibility for issuing all visas to aliens overseas. The Department of Justice (INS) is involved at ports of entry within the U.S. and, in fact, the Attorney General (Head of the Department of Justice) controls administration and enforcement of the INA.

In general, Congress has assigned responsibility for the definition of those medical conditions which are excludable to the Secretary of the Department of Health and Human Services, who has delegated this responsibility to the Public Health Service, Centers for Disease Control (CDC), Division of Quarantine. In addition to defining the conditions falling under each of the excludable categories, the CDC develops and administers guidelines and regulations governing medical processing for admission. The latest version of the "Guidelines for Medical Examination of Aliens" was issued in January 1987.

The examination and acceptance of individual aliens is conducted overseas at this time; in previous years the medical examination of aliens seeking entry to this country was performed at the port of entry. Ellis Island was previously one of the locations at which medical excludability was established. The transfer of this function to overseas has reduced the human and financial shortcomings of this arrangement, which led to last minute exclusions, separation of families, and long return journeys.

The medical exclusions apply similarly to all aliens seeking legal entry into the U.S. In practice, however, non-immigrants are not routinely required to have a complete medical examination, unless the consular officer has reason to believe it advisable. Further, any INS official at a port of entry can also detain any alien for medical examination at the port. An appeal process exists for medical conditions noted at ports of entry (Sec. 234).

The admission of persons with certain medically excludable conditions is permitted under waiver provisions, designed to facilitate family reunification. These provisions relate to persons who have certain relatives who are citizens, aliens admitted for permanent residence, or aliens issued immigrant visas. The waivers relate to mentally retarded persons, and persons with tuberculosis. Persons with a history of "mental illness" may be admitted if they are free of symptoms for a significant period (currently one year of stability or free of symptoms). Refugees alone, however, are covered by a generous authority of the Attorney General to waive any medical exclusion for "humanitarian purposes, to assure family unity, or when it is otherwise in the public interest."

The most recent major alteration in the medically excludable conditions occurred in 1987, with the addition of AIDS and AIDS virus positive to the list of dangerous contagious diseases. The list of excludable contagious diseases previously included several sexually transmitted diseases, including untreated syphilis, as well as infectious tuberculosis and Hansen's disease, or leprosy.

In Early 1987, government attention focused on the issue of AIDS and Immigration Policy. The U.S. Congress directed that AIDS would become an excludable condition by the end of August, 1987. Accordingly, AIDS became a part of the list of excludable contagious diseases effective August 31. After intensive debate and discussion, and seeking public comment, a positive AIDS antibody status was also added to the list of medically excludable conditions, effective December 1, 1987. That is, individuals who showed evidence of having been infected by the AIDS virus, whether they were ill or not would be excluded from entry into the U.S. Again, this provision is applicable to all individuals seeking legal entry into the Country, although tests are not routinely required of individuals seeking non-immigrant entry.

At the time of this writing, it is the position of INS that waivers of excludability due to AIDS will not be granted.

This was enacted since:

The science base presently requires that we assume all such persons are potentially infectious to others; and

Since, a significant percentage of those infected progress to serious illness or death. Several provisions of the regulations governing Aids examination should be noted:

All such examinations must be performed overseas, prior to arrival at a port of entry to the U.S.;

A positive antibody status must be confirmed by two Elisa tests and confirmed by a Western Blot test;

The regulation requires counselling be provided to individuals with a positive test; and that privacy of test results be maintained.

20

Migrant Health Program Strategic Work Plan, 1988-1991

SONIA M. LEON REIG
Director, U.S. Public Health Service, Bureau of Health Care Delivery and Assistance Migrant Health Program.

BACKGROUND

THE staff of the Migrant Health Branch, Division of Primary Care Services, Bureau of Health Care Delivery and Assistance have identified a number of strategic objectives which require priority attention over the next three years. This workplan was formulated within the context of the Fiscal Year 1988 Primary Care Management Strategy developed by DPCS and seeks to compliment rather than duplicate our combined efforts to provide improved primary care services to migrants and seasonal farmworkers and their families.

A number of people have been involved in developing the plan, including regional personnel, grantees, contractors, organizations, etc.

PURPOSE:

- Program guide;
- To direct program efforts, allocate resources and assign responsibilities of activities for timely performance;
- This is in addition to routine work activities.

USERS:

- Intended primarily as input to the working planning process for central office staff;
- Regional office staff, Migrant Health Centers, contractors and other organizations involved in the Migrant Health Program will also participate.

UPDATE:

- Plan will periodically be reviewed and revised.

PROGRAM GOAL:

- The goal of the Migrant Health Program is to improve the health status of MSFWs and their families.

MAJOR ASSUMPTIONS:

Financial
- funding level of $45 million
- 90-95% for maintenance of existing systems of care

Population Specific
- MSFWs are at greater risk than other working populations due to environmental, living conditions and lifestyle.
- Difficult to access services due to barriers of culture, language, economics, etc.

Current System
- Population is highly mobile
- Agriculture patterns impact the numbers, location and mix in streams
- Existing systems not responsive to needs
- Utilization episodic, continuity of care is difficult
- Provider recruitment difficult
- Majority of providers have had little experience with specialized health care needs of MSFWs.

WORKPLAN THEMES:

1. Access to Care
2. Integration and coordination of services
3. Improved communications

ORGANIZATION:

Under each theme there are a number of specific objectives with activity, timetable and products required to fulfill the objectives.

TOOLS TO BE USED TO ACHIEVE OBJECTIVES:

1. State Profiles
2. Need/Demand Assessments
3. Health Care Plans
4. BCRR Data
5. Epidemiological Profiles of MSFWs
6. Financial Assessments

THEME I Access to Care

Objective 1

To increase access to and availability of primary care services to the maximum extent to unserved areas indentified through State Profile Data and other information. Purpose here is to increase access and availability of existing health care resources to MSFWs in areas where the Migrant Health Program currently has no presence.

Objective 2

To set standards for all MHC to reach appropriate national market penetration rates (Migrant - Seasonal). This is designed to set standards for market penetration for each health delivery model of existing MHCs. For purposes of accountability each MHC must promote the availability of health services to the maximum number possible proportion of the target population.

Objective 3

To increase access to care in all MHCs which fall into the lowest quartile of achievement with respect to the appropriate standard penetration rate. Once a standard of performance has been set for existing MHCs, efforts should be made to make care accessible to the maximum intent possible. Program development will focus on eliminating barriers to care and increasing available options to reach the target population.

Objective 4

To reorient the system to provide more appropriate services to migrant and seasonal farmworkers, *e.g.* environmental and prevention. This objective attempts to close the gap between actual and perceived needs of MSFWs. Services would be based on current information collected and analyzed to determine accurately the status of factors influencing the health and welfare of MSFWs. The end result would be the ability to place program emphasis on current issues impacting on the target population in a more responsive and effective manner rather than to react in a delayed manner as in the past.

This objective can only be accomplished within the framework of a partnership between the MHP and the Regional Offices. To implement this objective training will be conducted on two levels; the Regional Office and Migrant Health Center staffs.

Objective 5

To encourage the development of Self-Help component to all MHC health promotion programs:

The Self-Help movement is gaining greater acceptance by the health care industry as an adjunct to medical practice and a tool for health promotion. On September 20, 1987, the Surgeon General held a workshop on creating a partnership between Self-Help and public health and endorsed collaborative efforts.

Our aim in this objective is to provide centers with direction and information such that they can effectively intitiate appropriate Self-Help activities with their clients.

Objective 6

To develop regional/state epidemiological profiles based on Health Care Plans and Need Demand Assessment:

We need to position ourselves into a modality of more aggressive interventions that will minimize preventable diseases and reduce the prevalance of chronic disease. More thoughtful analysis of the epidemiology of the populations currently served is necessary so we can adequately plan for services and comprehensively develop structured clinical responses.

Objective 7

To improve capabilities for early detection of shifting patterns of Migrant and Seasonal Farmworkers distribution and employment.

THEME 2: Maximize the Effectiveness of Comprehensive Service Delivery to MSFWs Through Increased Integration and Coordination with Existing Services

Objective 1

This objective has a two fold aim: to foster the provision of care to MSFWs in UNSERVED areas through existing health care providers in a coordinated manner and assure the delivery of comprehensive health care in SERVED areas by fostering greater coordination between MHC's and other service providers.

Objective 2

To provide investment opportunity funding for innovative demonstrations of service integration: Our aim here is to improve health care delivery and, ultimately, health status by improving the relationships of the service delivery components, within the MHC, among MHCs and other providers and within the streams.

Objective 3

To promote a balance of clinical and administrative input in program management and planning: Historically, the management of MHCs has been predominately influenced by administration. This administrative dominance was the logical result of the historical development of most MHCs as grass roots organizations, the directives of BHCDA regarding the BCRR and the temporary tenure of most providers in the MHCs.

The MHP has grown to the point where greater clinical involvement is imperative for the continued growth and development of the Program. The aim of this objective is to begin to create an appropriate balance between administrative and clinical influence in program planning and management. To this end the central office will continue to assure that all actions, guidances, policies, and efforts will have clinical input and will encourage the regional offices to do the same.

Objective 4

To promote grower involvement in issues which affect MSFW health status: Growers have significant influence on the lives of migrant and seasonal farmworkers. The aim of this objective is to turn more growers into supports of the needs of MSFWs by involving them in the problem solving process. We want to encourage more grower in the solutions for improving health status of migrant and seasonal farmworkers.

THEME 3: COMMUNICATIONS

Objective 1

To establish a common understanding of the Migrant Health Program: This objective attempts to raise the consciousness and knowledge about migrant health and Migrant Health Program related issues, of those involved and responsible for the management and implementation of the MHP. Implementation of this objective will create a comprehensive knowledge base that will allow an effective and efficient environment among all MHP officials (Federal, pubic and private).

Objective 2

To involve the Regional Offices in the process of goal setting decision making and implementing the Migrant Health Program nationwide: This objective is intended to seek the expertise of Regional Office Migrant Health Program staff in making decisions that will affect the Migrant Health Program. Accomplishment of this objective will build a cooperative network among Central Office and Regional Office Migrant Health Program staff.

Objective 3

To provide appropriate technical assistance to the Regional Migrant Health Program: This objective seeks to provide Regional Migrant Health Program staff with the proper assistance and/or resources that will achieve improved and successful program implementation.

Objective 4

To select one of the existing Migrant Health Regional Program Leads as the Lead RPC: There is a need for a Migrant Health Program Lead to frequently provide a regional office perspective on issues of Central Office and regional office interaction, MHP strategy development, and improved communications.

Objective 5

To foster replication of Central Office Interagency Committee on Migrants' meetings within each Region: This objective will create a network for the identification of those areas where federal programs can coordinate their services to better serve MSFWs.

Objective 6

To develop a formal Migrant Health Program recognition program: This objective seeks to provide a means to give formal recognition to Migrant Health Programs and/or staff that have performed effective and succesful activities in carrying out mission of the Migrant Health Program.

Objective 7

To develop and disseminate systematic documentation of MHP progress in achieving national goals and objectives: The purpose of this objective is to formally provide feedback on the accomplishments of the identified activities to those involved in implementation of the MHP Workplan. This type of information is valuable for decision making and future planning.

Objective 8

To develop contingency planning and quick response capability for all levels of Migrant Health Program management: The challenge ahead is in the implementation of the plan.

The result will be the improvement in the health of hundreds of migrant and seasonal farmworkers.

21

Migrant Clinician Network

JOHN W. MCFARLAND
Chair, Migrant Clinicians Network

THE Migrant Clinicians Network, essentially, is comprised of all providers who practice in migrant health centers.

The Migrant Clinicians Network was established to identify and address issues, which impact the health status of migrant and seasonal farmworkers, and to assess, and modify where necessary, the current health care delivery system to meet better the needs of this population. The Network, furthermore, serves as a national clinical forum for migrant and seasonal farmworker health issues. The Network functions as a resource for clinicians, migrant health centers, allied public and private agencies, and the migrant health program at the local, regional, and central office level.

The Network provides a nucleus for clinical representation among the 120 migrant health centers in the country (There are 120 migrant health centers with 400 sites. Eighty-six centers have in-house dental. These serve an estimated three million migrant and seasonal farmworkers, providing for a 17 percent penetration of the population).

Historically, the initial planning for the formation of the MCN occurred in Charleston, South Carolina, in 1984, with the idea of establishing a group of clinical providers responsive to the unique health care needs of the migrant and seasonal farmworker populations. Prior to the 8th Annual Migrant Health Conference held in Seattle, Washington, several individuals from various disciplines planned the formulation of a Network and scheduled a health care provider meeting to be held concurrently with the Health Conference. During that meeting the structure of the Network was established by regional representation. The Network addressed the Migrant Task Force on relevant clinical issues and goals during the 8th Annual Conference.

The first formal meeting of the Migrant Clinicians Network convened in Austin, Texas, on December 9th and 10th, 1985. The meeting was facilitated by the assistance of the National Migrant Referral Project and the Office of Migrant Health (BHCDA). The Network, as a group has met on five separate occasions. The formalized organizational structure was presented and approved at the Annual Meeting in Minneapolis in 1986. The basis used for structuring the Network evolved from the migration patterns found in the country. These include the three basic streams, Western, Midwestern, and Eastern. Migrant Health Centers located within each stream are divided into upstream and downstream programs and the Network has representation from each of the six regions.

STRUCTURE AND INTERAGENCY RELATIONSHIPS

How does the structure both within the Network and as the Network relate to other organizations? The Network itself is comprised of an executive committee of five members and six stream co-ordinators, two from each of the three streams. The Network is multidisciplinary and representative of various practice models within Migrant Health Centers including Centers with comprehensive service capability all the way to nursing-only models. Additionally, resource individuals serve periodically on current issues being addressed by the Network (An example would be the work of pharmacists Marsha Alvarez and Jan Perry in developing the formulary).

The Network is either working with or desirous of working with other agencies such as NMRP (which provides excellent staff support), NACHC, and the National Rural Health Association to further the cause of migrant health.

The charge of the Migrant Clinicians Network for the short run is to identify and address specific concerns about the provision of health care to the migrant and seasonal farmworker population and to effect positive change or modifications in the health care delivery system through "do-able" tasks. For the long term, the migrant clinicians network will address the issues of migrant clinical research, promote "conscience level raising" of the general population and the overall medical community about this underserved population. The network will serve as a resource of migrant health information, and promote a system of integrated health care access to migrant and seasonal farmworkers and their families.

Although the Network is in its infancy, it is a worthwhile concept whose time has come. It is bouyed by several factors which give it strength including:

• A good mix of disciplines and regional representation as well as dedicated, talented, and energetic individuals serving on the Network;

• Good support from the Office of Migrant Health and excellent staff support from NMRP;

• An agenda which is full, promising, interesting, and challenging; and

• A forum which gives clinical input into migrant health care delivery system.

ACCOMPLISHMENTS

The uniform formulary was developed with the intention of improving the uniformity of chronic care medications which are prescribed up and down the streams. The idea is to assist patients and reduce confusion regarding medications. The formulary will be updated semi-annually and the Migrant Clinicians Network will advocate for provider consensus. In the future, a uniform formulary could possibly facilitate bulk purchasing and reduced costs for medications.

The Network is developing a set of chronic care guidelines or treatment protocols for targeted disease entities which show a high incidence in migrant and seasonal farmworker populations. The original guidelines were developed by Dale Benson of the Neighborhood Health Centers of Indianapolis, Indiana, and are being modified to meet the unique situations encountered in Migrant Health Centers in treating migrant and seasonal farmworkers. The modification is entitled the "CLEF" process which stands for C, cultural; L, language; E, environmental and educational; and F, follow-up. Additionally, the CLEF process is keyed to the SOAP process or subjective, objective, assessment, and plan, used in protocol development. All of this is done to provide a meaningful protocol which can be practically applied by health providers in Migrant Health Centers.

We are currently preparing an orientaton package for clinicians practicing in Migrant Health Centers. Written by anthropologist, Bob Trotter. It isized the approach which makes the document effective and appealing to health care providers. Additionally, the Network plans to develop audio visual orientation packages of varying lengths for different situations such as full time providers and part time providers, as well as students, interns, and residents practicing in Migrant Health Centers.

The Network is currently in the process of developing the Migrant Clinicians Resource Manual which would serve as a compendium to include the formulary, the provider orientation package, and the chronic care guidlines, as well as clinical supplements, bibliographies and resources as they become available.

As far as consortia development or collaborative strategies, the Network is working to develop arrangements between Migrant Health Centers and schools of medicine, nursing, and dentistry for the purpose of expanding health care services to our patients. These arrangements have many advantages including:

•   Opportunities to expose health care provider students to Migrant Health Centers and encourage these students to consider career opportunities in migrant health;

•   Opportunities for providers to assist in the teaching and training of students, interns, and residents;

- Development of relationships between Migrant Health Centers and schools of medicine, nursing, and dentistry to the mutual benefit of all;
- Increased services to migrant and seasonal farmworkers and their families; and
- Improved cost effectiveness in providing these services.

It should be added that such programs are one of the most effective means of teaching social awareness issues to future health care providers.

The Migrant Health Newsline is a publication of the National Migrant Referral Project and the Network is acting as an Editorial Board and providing authors from within and outside the Network for clinical supplements to the Newsletter.

Members of the Network have provided clinical testimony for legislative bodies both at the state and federal level.

The Network will begin the process of developing and establishing a national migrant research agenda.

As far as additional accomplishments, the Network has supplied copies of the Mexican PDR to the Migrant Health Centers; the Network has provided family planning educational materials for migrant and seasonal farmworkers; the Network assists with the planning of the Migrant Health Conference; and the Network participates in the medical alert system.

ROLE

The role of the Migrant Clinicians Network includes the following:
- To act as a nucleus of health care providers which reviews, shares, and disseminates information;
- To promote and facilitate networking among Migrant Health Centers and assist in the coordination of efforts and resources with other public and private agencies;
- To promote and facilitate informal and formal consortia development;
- To advocate for migrant health issues at all levels, public and private;
- To provide formal and informal education on topics involving migrant health status and the provision of health care;
- To provide a forum for problem-solving for migrant clinical issues, and to act as a catalyst for implementing solutions to clinical problems.
- To serve as a migrant clinical resource and provide relevant clinical expertise;
- To promote the utilization of Migrant Health Centers as educational health care settings and encourage recruitment of health care students into Migrant Health Centers;
- To provide clinical management input and direction to the migrant program at the regional and federal level;
- To develop a Migrant Health Research Agenda for the purpose of identifying and quantifying health care problems with the ultimate goal of improving migrant health status;

- To develop clinical strategies and protocols to positively impact on the quality of care to migrant and seasonal farmworkers and their families; and
- To further advocate for services not defined in the traditional medical model which are required for the provision of quality health care in this population. Examples of those services include patient transportation, outreach, social service linkages and coordination, and environmental and occupational health.

FUTURE AREAS OF CONCENTRATION FOR THE NETWORK

Among future areas of concentration for the Network are the following:
- Establishment of a society for migrant research, a multidisciplinary society with strong academic ties and a yearly research symposium;
- Establishment of a migrant health course in a major public health hospital;
- Addressing the perplexing problem of effective medical information transfer which has, to date, not been successfully achieved.;
- Documentation of the clinical impact of occupational and sanitation problems in the migrant and seasonal farmworker populations;
- The formation of a Migrant Clinical Resource Center through the National Migrant Referral Project with clinically relative publications to benefit clinicians in Migrant Health Centers;
- An audiovisual library of migrant farmworker health care issues including formalized slide presentations and VCR videos;
- Yearly updates of current clinical initiatives such as the guidelines and the formulary;
- Assist in the development of accurate morbidity and mortality reporting in the migrant and seasonal farmworker population; and
- Greater participation with professional academic institutions in medicine, nursing, and dentistry directly and through such programs as AHEC.

22

The Impact of the New Immigration Law on Education

SYLVIA M. ROBERTS AND IRENE J. WILLIS
New Jersey State Department of Education

IMMIGRATION policy and implementation, whether exclusionary and tightly controlled, broadly inclusive and loosely administered — or, as is more often the case, somewhere on a continuum between those extremes — always has an impact on education. It affects the numbers entering our schools and the rate at which they enter; it affects the number, nature and quality of services offered to immigrant children and their parents as well as to those who were here before them; and it affects the physical and economic well-being of children and their parents. It profoundly affects the quality of life of the families of immigrant school-age children and, thereby, the climate of the schools they attend and the effectiveness with which those schools can do the job the public schools are supposed to do — educate all the children of all the people as thoroughly and efficiently as possible.

What effect will IRCA have? Will it make things better or worse for immigrants — easier or more difficult to educate their children?

It is reasonable to assume that many of the illegal aliens currently living in this country have school-age children — that among the children in our schools, particularly in our bilingual, English as a second language, and migrant programs are those whose parents are illegal aliens. Estimates are that there are hundreds of thousands of such children in the nation's public schools (First, J.M. and Carrera, J.W., 1988).

But we don't know who they are. And, as educators, we need not know who they are. That's not our job. Our job is to see to it that all children get the best education we have the resources to give them — to enroll and teach those who arrive at schoolhouse doors. In *Plyler v. Doe*, 457 U.S.202 (1982) the Supreme Court ruled that no child may be refused enrollment in a public school solely on the basis of the child's or the parents' immigration status. Nor may a state withold funds from local districts for admitting the children of illegal aliens (First, J.M. and Carrera, J.W., 1988).

So, if we need not know which of our children have parents who are illegal immigrants, and if we are already teaching all the children that come to us to be taught, how does IRCA affect those of us who are educators? What is its educational impact?

Let's look first at the obvious impact. Interpreting the law most literally, IRCA affects us primarily as employers (Goodis, 1986). An educational agency, whether public or private, elementary, secondary or collegiate level; local, state or federal in its operation, has the same obligation as any employer to require, of any new hire, evidence of legal status. In many of our urban districts, the school system is the largest single employer in the community. In addition to regularly employed certificated staff and long- and short-term substitutes, a school district may be the employer of aides, teaching assistants, outside consultants and other contract employees such as coaches and directors of special programs; as well as custodians, cafeteria workers, secretaries, clerks, crossing guards, and attendance officers.

As any employer must, the school district or other educational agency must question the legal status of all new employees. The school or other educational agency is no more responsible than other employers for verifying the authenticity of the documentation provided, nor does it have the capacity to do so (Federal Register, 1985).

The responsibility of a state educational agency is broader than that of a school district, however. Not only is it an employer of many people with diverse functions, but it is also:

1. a certifier of courses designed to prepare eligible aliens for status adjustment (Schuman, 1987);

2. a coordinator for the review and approval of applications for federal funds designated for programs of assistance to certain categories of immigrants — refugees, for example, and those granted asylum status — and for educational organizations impacted by these categories (United States Department of Education, 1988);

3. a monitor of compliance with federal and state guidelines and regulations covering such programs (United States Department of Education, 1988); and

4. an explainer, adviser, and interpreter for school personnel trying to understand their roles and responsibilities and to carry them out conscientiously. For example, we have recently advised school districts that they may, with the alien's written consent, release the Multiple Student Record Transfer Systems (MSRTS) record for use in documenting continuous residence in the United States (Staehle, 1987).

These aspects are the obvious, first line of educational impact of IRCA. But there are also other, less obvious ways in which immigration policy affects education.

No one knows with any degree of certainty how many illegal aliens there are in the United States. Estimates vary widely (First, J.M. and Carrera, J.W.,

1988). What we do know, however, is that many of the estimates previously accepted have failed to take into consideration the fact that the *net* flow of undocumented aliens, is always less than the *gross* flow (Gann, L.H. and Duignan, P.J., 1986).

This mobility of the illegal alien population may be one of the hidden variables affecting education right now — impacting on enrollment, attendance and dropout rates; the level, amount, quality and type of parent involvement, — all of which affect student achievement.

This is not to say that we are satisfied with the attendance and dropout rates of our native-born students, nor with the level of involvement of their parents. But, for the immigrant child, the legal or illegal status of the parents affects the way both the child and the parents feel about the school, a structure of authority in the society. A well-meant question from a teacher, school official or social worker can trigger fear in an immigrant youngster and his or her family — fear of deportation, of separation from family members, of having to make the difficult choice between accepting needed social services and thereby perhaps jeopardizing legalization status, or of sacrificing the short-term welfare of the family for the long-term goal of status adjustment. Fear and anxiety in the family means fear and anxiety in the child. A frightened, anxious child finds learning more difficult.

Immigration experts report that illegal aliens are often reluctant to seek any kind of medical or dental treatment, for fear of being found out and deported. Although Medicaid services are available to their children under eighteen and to pregnant women, the families may still be reluctant to seek such services — with unfortunate consequences for the children, for future children, and for the education of those children (*CDF Reports*, 1987).

With the exception of Cuban-Haitian entrants, immigrants who have applied for permanent legal status are barred from most federally funded public assistance programs during their five-year wait for permanent legal status, although some emergency services may be provided. If their children are United States citizens and those children receive public benefits, the parents' status adjustment may be in jeopardy. If eligible legalized aliens accept food stamps or AFDC funds during the waiting time for permanent legal status, they may jeopardize their status. If their children accept student financial aid to attend college, those children may never be able to gain permanent legal status (*CDF Reports*, 1987). An unhealthy child, a badly nourished child, a child who doesn't believe studying will lead to a better future and those parents are reluctant to apply even for social benelfits for which they are eligible, is a child who is difficult to educate.

Does immigration policy affect education? It certainly does. As we have seen, it affects:

• student enrollment, and as a consequence, school facilities, staffing, programming, scheduling, and class size;

- student mobility;
- parent involvement;
- curriculum;
- instruction;
- drop-out and graduation rates;
- attendance;
- student emotional and physical health;
- the availability of aides, teaching assistants and other school personnel;
- the guidance function;
- school record-keeping requirements;
- the economic status of students and their families, and student eligibility
for certain federally assisted educational programs;
- staff development needs;
- the demographics of the school population; and
- access to higher education for the children of immigrants.

IRCA 1986 represents the first major change in immigration law in over thirty years (Goodis, 1986). We can surmise, therefore, that among the variables affecting education at present, particularly in our urban schools, are those having to do with previous immigration law and its enforcement.

As we have already seen, a school district is an employer — and as an employer is subject to the same penalties as any other for knowingly hiring illegal aliens. This obviously affects all aspects of personnel administration — recruitment, recordkeeping and the general availability of employable personnel. Certain categories of school workers — aides, teaching assistants, office and cafeteria staff, custodial staff — are frequently recruited from immigrant populations. These workers are most likely to be affected by the new law, as are certain programs. Those programs most likely to require the hiring of people with language backgrounds other than English — migrant, bilingual and ESL programs, for example — may be, more heavily impacted than others. The pool of potential workers in these categories may decline as a result of IRCA. However, because of IRCA's requirement that candidates for permanent legalization either: 1) demonstrate English language skills and knowledge of United States history; or 2) be enrolled in an approved educational program (Schuman, 1987), the knowledge and skill level of that pool of potential workers may be higher than it has been in recent years.

Student enrollment impact is less readily discernible, but one state that appears to have already experienced such impact is California. Los Angeles area staff officials in 1987-88 enrolled fewer than half the number of new students anticipated. The Superintendent of Schools attributes the decline to fear of deportation and possibly to the fear of having families split apart. Some students may also have left school, he speculates further, to earn the $400 needed to apply for amnesty. The Los Angeles Unified School District, the nation's second largest, lost $27 million in state aid based on average daily attendance, because only 2,000 new students enrolled instead of the 14,000 expected. Similar results were found in Los Angeles county (Jennings, 1988).

Although Texas has not experienced an enrollment decrease this year, officials speculate that any potential decline might have been offset by their new statewide pre-kindergarten program (Jennings, 1988).

In Florida, an enrollment increase of 67,000 is anticipated because of the special immigration status granted to Cuban citizens by the United States government (Jennings, 1988).

New Jeresey has not yet experienced any enrollment surges or declines traceable to IRCA, and it is difficult to say whether we will. According to INS data, the 9,681 regular provisional legalization applications received in New Jersey through January 7, 1988, 940 were for children aged 6-17. Eight school-age children were represented among the Seasonal Agricultural Worker (SAW) applications.

The nationality groups presenting the greatest number of applications as of January 1988 were:

Colombia	984
Philippines	880
Poland	789
El Salvador	775
Haiti	719
Mexico	601
Peru	523
Ecuador	406

The greatest concentration by age group — 3,127 of the total — was between the ages of 25 and 34 (INS, 1988). These are peak years for childbearing and child-rearing.

The pattern, historically, among our immigrant population in New Jersey has been that as the adults settle in and become gainfully employed, they send for the rest of their families. Since first priority is given to children and spouses, if each applicant brings only one more person, the probability is that several thousand of the new arrivals will be school-age children.

But of course, it will be another five years before the eligible legalized aliens are adjusted to permanent legal status. During their "wait time" much can happen to affect their futures. The next few years will continue to be a period of great uncertainty and anxiety for the families involved.

The tighter immigration policy represented by IRCA will probably bring about a shift in both numbers of students and the characteristics of students in programs affected most strongly by immigration — migrant, bilingual, and ESL.

If immigration becomes more controlled and orderly, the nature of some of our educational programs may change. Our emphasis may be less on how to deal with huge numbers and more on how to serve the existing population better.

We may also have the security of knowing that the vast majority of students in these programs are legal residents of the United States and therefore eligible for whatever public benefits they have need of, including financial assistance in attending college.

Our attendance and graduation rates will almost certainly improve when students are able to leave their "shadow world", as it has been called, and enter mainstream society.

And, hopefully, their parents will have less fear of contact with the school and all that it represents. They may come to see the school as an accessible resource rather than a threat to their survival in this country.

To summarize, although the most obvious effect of IRCA on the educational agency is on its role as employer, immigration law — whether inclusive, exclusionary, or somewhere on a continuum between these extremes — affects many other aspects of education. The specific impact of IRCA has been felt most strongly so far in Southern California, where enrollment has declined suddenly and severely, but it may have different effects in other parts of the United States. If immigration becomes more controlled, we may be able to serve more effectively the existing population of immigrant students. We can anticipate improvement in distribution of public benefits, in attendance and graduation rates, and in parent involvement in the schools.

REFERENCES

Federal Register, 50(158): 2563. August 13, 1985

First, J.M. and Carrera, J.W. New Voices: Immigrant Students in United States Public Schools. Boston, Massachusetts: National Coalition of Advocates for Students, 1988.

Gann, L.H. and Duignan, P.J. The Hispanics in the United States: A History. Boulder, Colorado: Westview Press, Inc., Frederick A. Praeger, Publisher, 1986; and Stanford, California: The Hoover Institution on War, Revolution and Peace, 1986.

Goodis, T.A. "A Layman's Guide to 1986 United States Immigration Reform". Washington, D.C.: The Urban Institute, 1986.

"Immigration and Naturalization Service Statistical Data", January 1988. (Taken from INS tapes and tabulated by the United States Department of Health and Human Services; distributed to state educational agencies as Data Bits, January 1988.)

Jennings, L. "Enrollment Decline in Los Angeles Tied to New United States Immigration Law". Education Week, April 20, 1988.

"The New Immigration Law and Public Benefits: Questions and Answers" CDF Reports, 9(2), July 1987. Washington, D.C.: Children's Defense Fund, July 1987.

Schuman, J. "Legalization: Phase Two. Requirements and Guidelines to Courses of Study Recognized by the Attorney General". Washington, D.C.: United States Immigration and Naturalization Service, 1987.

Staehle, J.F. "Memorandum to Chief State School Officers". Washington, D.C.: Office of Migrant Education, United States Office of Education, [1987#.

"State Legalization Impact Assistance Grants: Program Description". Washington, D.C.: *United States Department of Education*, February 26, 1988.

EPILOGUE

In acceptance of CMS Immigration and Refugee Policy Award

MARION M. DAWSON

MADAME Chair, Bishop Haines, Fathers Tomasi, Ladies and Gentlemen:

We are honored to receive this award and accept it, not on our own behalf, but on behalf of the two groups of Americans who have truly earned it:

First, our national and regional staffs and the thousands of members of our churches and organizations and their friends and communities across this great nation who have welcomed refugees, reached out to immigrants, and cared for undocumented migrants since the beginning - the beginning being really more than two hundred years ago.

Second, the refugees, immigrants, displaced persons, asylum seekers, migrants from across the globe — aliens all — whom it has been our privilege to serve.

We do believe our nation knows its finest hours when it reaches out to embrace those from other lands who seek freedom and an opportunity for a viable life, a life which upholds their individual human dignity. Those who welcome refugees, promoting justice to even the least fortunate, serve the cause of world peace, thinking perhaps that there, but for the grace of God and those who welcomed their ancestors, go they. They also learn that Americans who dare show love to "the stranger and the sojourner in our midst" are mightily blessed in return.

Why else would we, that peculiar group of twelve national refugee resettlement voluntary agencies who form what is known to some as the InterAction Migration and Refugee Committee, but to others the Refugee, Inc. Cartel, go on? Why else would we colleagues, some of whose names appear in your program, others whose do not but perhaps should, continue to harangue and challenge U.S. government leaders, departmental officials, and Congressional representatives to be more generous?

In the process, we have earned at least one interesting nickname I have heard in the hallowed chambers on C Street, and that is "The Dirty Dozen"!

Why would we go on? Because we and those we represent are schooled by and spiritually uplifted by the foreign born we have welcomed, whose strength and courage far exceeds our own, replenishing the national will to stand for what is humane, for what is right.

And so, we fervently pray, will it continue.

APPENDIX

Program of the CMS Eleventh Annual National Legal Conference on Immigration and Refugee Policy

Sponsored by:
The Center for Migration Studies of New York, Inc. at the
Grand Hyatt, Washington, D.C.
April 21-22, 1988

Program
THURSDAY, APRIL 21, 1988

7:45-8:45	FINAL REGISTRATION
8:45 a.m. - 9:00 a.m.	WELCOME
	Lydio F. Tomasi, c.s., Executive Director, The Center for Migration Studies

9:00 a.m.   **SESSION I: IMPLEMENTING THE IMMIGRATION REFORM AND CONTROL ACT OF 1986 (IRCA)**

Chair: **Austin T. Fragomen, Jr.,** Esq., Fragomen, Del Rey & Bernsen

Opening Remarks: **The Hon. Alan Nelson,** I.N.S. Commissioner

A) LEGALIZATION

Panelists: **William Slattery,** I.N.S. Assistant Commissioner for Legalization
Ira J. Kurzban, President, American Immigration Lawyers Association
Walter Barnes, Chief, Office of Refugee Services, State of California

Reactors: **Gilbert Carrasco,** Esq., USCC Migration & Refugee Services
Doris Meissner, Carnegie Endowment for International Peace
Howard R. Rosenberg, University of California at Berkeley

DISCUSSION

10:45 - 11:00 a.m.   COFFEE BREAK

B) SANCTIONS AND DISCRIMINATION

Panelists: **Arnold Jones,** Senior Associate Director, G.A.O.
Lawrence Siskind, Special Counsel for Discrimination, U.S. Department of Justice
John F. Shaw, I.N.S. Assistant Commissioner for Investigations
Virginia Lamp-Thomas, Esq., U.S. Chamber of Commerce

Reactors: **Wade Henderson,** Esq., American Civil Liberties Union
Robert L. Bach, State University of New York at Binghamton

DISCUSSION

12:30 p.m. - 2:00 p.m.   AWARDS LUNCHEON PROGRAM

Presiding: **The Hon. Donna M. Alvarado,** Director, ACTION

Benediction: **Right Rev. Ronald H. Haines, D.D.,** Episcopal Church, Washington, D.C.

Speaker: **The Hon. Charles E. Schumer,** U.S. House of Representatives

Honorees: **Marion Dawson,** Migration Affairs, Protestant Episcopal Church in the U.S.A.
Dale S. DeHaan, Church World Service Immigration and Refugee Programs
Donald G. Hohl, USCC Migration and Refugee Services
Donald H. Larson, Lutheran Immigration and Refugee Services
Leon Marion, Tolstoy Foundation
Karl D. Zukerman, The Hebrew Immigration Aid Society

2:00 p.m. - 5:00 p.m.   ## SESSION II: BEYOND I.R.C.A.: CURRENT LEGISLATIVE INITIATIVES

Chair: **CharlesB.Keely,**DonaldG.HerzbergChairinInternationalMigration,GeorgetownUniversity

Opening Remarks: **The Hon. Romano Mazzoli,** U.S. House of Representatives

Panelists: **Richard Day,** Minority Counsel, Sucommittee on Immigration and Refugee Policy, U.S. Senate
Jerry Tinker, Staff Director, Subcommittee on Immigration and Refugee Affairs,
Lawrence H. Fuchs, Brandeis University
H. Ronald Klasko, Esq., Abraham & Lowenstein, Philadelphia
John M. Goering, Commission for the Study of International Migration and Cooperative Development

Reactor: **Milton D. Morris,** Director of Research, Joint Center for Political Studies Washington, D.C.

DISCUSSION

6:00 p.m. - 9:00 p.m.   RECEPTION, Botanic Garden, U.S. Capitol

FRIDAY, APRIL 22, 1988

9:00 a.m. - 10:45 a.m.   ## SESSION III. REFUGEES

Chair: **David Martin,** University of Virginia School of Law

Opening Remarks: **Ambassador Johnathan Moore,** U.S. Coordinator for Refugee Affairs

Panelists: **Delia Combs,** I.N.S. Assistant Commissioner for Refugees Asylum and Parole
Arthur Helton, Lawyers Committee for Human Rights
Deborah Anker, Harvard Law School

Reactor: **Guy Goodwin-Gill,** UNHCR, Geneva

DISCUSSION

10:45 a.m. - 11:00 a.m.   COFFEE BREAK

11:00 a.m. - 1:00 p.m.   **SESSION IV: MIGRATION POLICY: HEALTH
AND EDUCATION**

Chair: **Roy S. Bryce-Laporte,** C.I.P.S., College of Staten Island, City University of New York

Panelists: **Carol R. Ausuble,** Milbank Memorial Fund
Joanne Luoto, Chief, Refugee Program, U.S. Public Health Service
Ron D'Alosio, Director, Farmworker Justice Fund, Washington, D.C.
Sonia Reig, Director, Migrant Health Program, Washington, D.C.
John McFarland, Chair, Migrant Clinicians Network
Sylvia Roberts, Division of Compensatory and Bilingual Education, New Jersey State Department of Education

DISCUSSION AND CONCLUSIONS

PROGRAM ORGANIZING COMMITTEE:

Lydio F. Tomasi, Chairman; Graziano Battistella; Austin T. Fragomen, Jr.; Charles B. Keely; Mark Miller; Maggie Sullivan; Silvano Tomasi.

Index